Disclaimer Notice:

This book is intended for educational and informational purposes only. While every effort has been made to ensure the accuracy and reliability of the information presented, it should not be considered as professional advice.

The author, an American writer, has based this book primarily on U.S. laws and practices. Legal, financial, and medical situations, divorce proceedings, and available resources can vary significantly in international jurisdictions. Readers outside the United States should be aware that the information provided may not fully apply to their specific country or region. Financial systems, healthcare practices, insurance policies, and social support structures differ widely across nations and may impact the applicability of advice given in this book.

The author does not render legal, financial, medical, or other professional services. The strategies and suggestions outlined in this book should not be used as a substitute for consultation with professional advisors familiar with your local laws, regulations, financial systems, and healthcare practices.

Readers are encouraged to seek the services of competent professionals in their respective countries for advice tailored to their specific situations, jurisdictions, and local systems. This includes lawyers, financial advisors, and healthcare providers who understand the nuances of your particular region.

The author and publisher disclaim any liability, loss, or risk incurred as a consequence, directly or indirectly, of the use and application of any of the contents of this book.

By reading this book, you acknowledge that the author cannot be held responsible for any losses or damages arising from the use of the information contained herein, including but not limited to errors, omissions, or inaccuracies, particularly in contexts outside the United States or in situations where local financial, legal, or medical practices differ significantly from those described in this book.

Copyright © 2024 by Gina Grant

All rights reserved.

No portion of this book may be reproduced in any form without written permission from the publisher or author, except as permitted by U.S. copyright law.

CONTENTS

Dedication — 1

Introduction — 2

1. Chapter 1 — 4
   Understanding Narcissistic Abuse

2. Chapter 2 — 17
   The Emotional Toll of Divorce from a Narcissist

3. Chapter 3 — 30
   Protecting Your Mental Health

4. Chapter 4 — 44
   Navigating the Legal Process

5. Chapter 5 — 58
   Financial Survival and Recovery

6. Chapter 6 — 84
   Co-Parenting with a Narcissist

7. Chapter 7 — 104
   Rebuilding Your Self-Esteem

8. Chapter 8 — 120
   Rediscovering Yourself

9. Chapter 9 — 142
   Healing and Moving Forward

10. Chapter 10 — 162
    Embracing Single Parenthood

Conclusion — 184

Additional Tools — 197

Glossary of Terms — 218

References — 224

To every brave soul who has felt lost, alone, or broken by narcissistic abuse

This book is a lifeline thrown to you with love

INTRODUCTION

Welcome to a community you never asked to join. By opening these pages, you've taken a crucial step in your journey through one of life's most daunting challenges: a divorce entangled with narcissistic abuse. Your presence here speaks volumes about your resilience and determination to reclaim your life. Take heart – in this book, you've found a new ally on your path to healing and empowerment.

This isn't just another self-help book, nor is it a substitute for professional help. Think of it as your cheerleader and BFF who's been there and gets it. It's a comforting voice in the dark, a shoulder to lean on, and a gentle nudge forward when you need it most.

"Divorcing a Narcissist? Your Cheery Companion Through Divorce and Beyond" is exactly what it says on the tin – a friendly, supportive companion on your path to recovery. It's a lifeline tossed with love, a rallying cry for your spirit, and a hand-drawn map to help you navigate the twists and turns of reclaiming your life after narcissistic abuse.

While this book doesn't replace the expertise of lawyers, therapists, accountants, or law enforcement officers, it offers something equally valuable:

- Strategies for understanding and healing from narcissistic abuse

- Practical tips for navigating the legal aspects of divorce

- Tools for rebuilding your self-esteem and rediscovering your identity

- Techniques for setting boundaries and protecting your mental health

- Insights on co-parenting with a narcissist

- A healthy dose of humor to lighten the journey

So, grab a cup of tea, settle into a comfy chair, and prepare to embark on a journey of healing and self-discovery. Remember, you're not alone in this journey. This book is here to be your companion and your guide as you navigate the path from survival to thriving. Let's take those first steps together towards a brighter, narcissist-free future.

CHAPTER 1

Understanding Narcissistic Abuse

DEFINING NARCISSISTIC PERSONALITY DISORDER

If you're reading this, chances are you've been through the wringer. Maybe you're still in it, fighting your way through a storm of confusion, hurt, and self-doubt. Here's something important to recognize right off the bat: You're not crazy. You're not overreacting. And you're definitely not alone.

Brace yourself as the curtain rises on the main character in your divorce drama – narcissistic personality disorder. It's a mouthful, isn't it? And it sounds like something straight out of a psychology textbook. But don't let the fancy term intimidate you. Understanding this concept is like finding the key to a door you've been banging your head against for far too long.

Narcissistic personality disorder (NPD) isn't just about someone who loves to stare at their reflection or posts too many selfies. We're talking about a serious mental health condition that can turn your world upside down if you're in a relationship with someone who has it.

So, what exactly is NPD? In a nutshell, it's a pattern of behavior where a person has an inflated sense of their own importance, a deep need for excessive attention and admiration, and a lack of empathy for others. But behind this mask of ultra-confidence lies a fragile self-esteem that's vulnerable to the slightest criticism.

Sounds familiar? Let's break it down a bit more.

People with NPD often:

1. Have an exaggerated sense of self-importance

2. Expect to be recognized as superior even without achievements that warrant it

3. Exaggerate their achievements and talents

4. Are preoccupied with fantasies about success, power, brilliance, beauty, or the perfect mate

5. Believe they are superior and can only be understood by or associate with equally special people

6. Require constant admiration

7. Have a sense of entitlement

8. Take advantage of others to get what they want

9. Have an inability or unwillingness to recognize the needs and feelings of others

10. Are envious of others and believe others envy them

11. Behave in an arrogant or haughty manner

You might be having an "aha" moment right now, thinking, "That describes my ex to a T!" or "This is exactly what I've been living with for years!" And you know what? Whether you're dealing with a former husband, wife, partner, or co-parent, recognizing the patterns of narcissistic behavior is crucial.

This moment of clarity, this recognition, is more than just an interesting observation. It's the beginning of your journey towards understanding, healing, and ultimately, freedom. It's the point where confusion starts to give way to comprehension, where self-doubt begins to transform into self-awareness.

People with NPD aren't usually aware that they have it. In their minds, they're not the problem – everyone else is. This lack of self-awareness is part of the disorder, and it's what makes it so challenging to deal with.

You might be wondering, "How did I end up here? I'm a smart, capable person. How did I not see this coming?" It's a common question, and the answer lies in understanding the nature of narcissistic behavior.

Narcissists are expert manipulators who have honed their skills over years and are often incredibly charming, especially at the beginning of a relationship. They're frequently described as charismatic, confident, and exciting. It's easy for anyone to get swept off their feet by such captivating personalities.

But as time goes on, the mask starts to slip. The charming prince or princess turns into a frog, but not overnight. It happens slowly, insidiously, until one day you wake up and wonder how your life turned into this emotional rollercoaster.

Narcissistic abuse can happen to anyone, regardless of how smart, strong, or capable they are. In fact, narcissists often target highly empathetic, successful people. Your big heart and accomplishments aren't weaknesses – they're strengths that someone chose to exploit. Many smart, successful people have found themselves in similar situations.

Understanding NPD is not about diagnosing your partner or ex-partner – that's a job for mental health professionals. It's about making sense of your experiences, validating your feelings, and starting to see clearly what's been happening in your relationship.

Remember, knowledge is power. The more you understand about narcissistic personality disorder, the better equipped you'll be to protect yourself, heal, and move forward. Ready to start this transformative journey? Let's turn the page together and begin your story of recovery and empowerment.

SIGNS AND PATTERNS OF NARCISSISTIC ABUSE IN RELATIONSHIPS

You're here because something in your relationship just doesn't feel right. Maybe you've been walking on eggshells, constantly second-guessing yourself, or feeling like you're on an emotional rollercoaster that never stops. You're not losing your mind – you might be experiencing narcissistic abuse.

It's natural to have doubts at this point. You might be thinking, "Abuse? But there was never any physical violence." Here's a crucial point to understand: abuse isn't always physical. Narcissistic abuse is like a stealth bomber – it flies under the radar, wreaking havoc on your self-esteem and sanity without leaving visible scars.

This form of abuse is often subtle, elusive, and can be hard to recognize, especially when you're in the midst of it. It doesn't leave bruises or broken bones, but its impact on your emotional and psychological well-being can be just as devastating, if not more so. Like a slow-acting poison, it gradually erodes your sense of self, your confidence, and your perception of reality.

So, what does this invisible warfare look like? Let's break it down:

1. The Jekyll and Hyde Act: Remember how charming your partner was at the beginning? That wasn't a fluke. Narcissists are often skilled practitioners of a manipulation tactic known as "love bombing." They shower you with attention, affection, and promises of a fairy-tale future. But once they've got you hooked, the façade crumbles. Suddenly, you're face-to-face with a stranger, wondering what cosmic switcheroo replaced the person you fell in love with.

2. Gaslighting Galore: Ever felt like you're losing your grip on reality? That's gaslighting in action. This term, derived from the

1938 stage play "Gas Light" which was adapted into a movie in 1944, refers to a form of psychological manipulation where the abuser attempts to sow seeds of doubt in the victim's mind, making them question their own memory, perception, and sanity. Your narcissistic partner might deny saying things you clearly remember, accuse you of overreacting, or flat-out tell you that your perception is wrong. It's crazy-making at its finest.

3. The Blame Game: In a narcissist's world, they're never at fault. Had a fight? It's because you're too sensitive. They cheated? You weren't attentive enough. This constant blame-shifting can leave you feeling like you're always walking on thin ice, constantly braced for the next accusation.

4. Emotional Rollercoaster: One minute they're singing your praises, the next they're tearing you down. This unpredictable behavior serves a calculated purpose. By keeping you in a constant state of emotional flux, they ensure your attention remains firmly fixed on them. You become so focused on anticipating their next mood swing that you lose sight of your own needs and well-being. This creates a cycle of dependency where you're perpetually off-balance, seeking their elusive approval and validation. It's a powerful control tactic that keeps you emotionally tethered, always hoping for the next high while bracing for the inevitable low.

5. Smear Campaigns: Narcissists are often charming in public but monsters behind closed doors. They might spread rumors about

you, turning friends and family against you. This isolation tactic makes you more dependent on them, shrinking your support network and amplifying their control.

6. Boundary Bulldozing: Say goodbye to personal space and privacy. A narcissist will trample all over your boundaries, whether it's reading your texts, controlling your finances, or deciding who you can and can't see. They act as if your personal space is their territory to control and expand into at will.

7. The Silent Treatment: Ah, the narcissist's favorite punishment. They'll give you the cold shoulder for days, leaving you anxious and desperate for their attention.

8. Triangulation: Ever feel like there's always a third person in your relationship? That's triangulation. They might flirt with others in front of you, compare you unfavorably to exes, or constantly bring up how much someone else admires them. This manipulative tactic creates a psychological love triangle, even if the third party is unaware of their role in this emotional shell game.

9. Financial Abuse: Money becomes a weapon. They might control all the finances, run up debts in your name, or use money to keep you dependent on them. This form of abuse may extend beyond immediate financial control, often having long-lasting implications on your economic future.

10. Hoovering: Just when you think you're out, they pull you back in. This could be through grand gestures, promises to change,

or playing on your sympathy. It's like a vacuum cleaner (hence the name) sucking you back into the cycle of abuse. Your ex might show up with grand gestures, promises of change, or an Oscar-worthy performance of remorse. They're playing on your hope, your need for closure, and your belief that people can change. It's a clever trick – they give you just enough space to feel free, then reel you back in when you're vulnerable.

These patterns often creep up so slowly that you don't realize how bad things have gotten until you're in deep. It's like the old analogy of a frog in boiling water. Throw a frog into boiling water, and it'll jump right out. But put it in cool water and slowly turn up the heat, and it'll stay put until it's too late.

You might be sitting there thinking, "Oh my god, that's my life." And you know what? That realization, as painful as it is, is incredibly powerful. Because once you can name it, once you can see the patterns, you can start to break free.

THE CYCLE OF NARCISSISTIC ABUSE

Picture this: you're on a merry-go-round that's spinning way too fast. You want to get off, but every time you try, something pulls you back in. Sound familiar? That's the cycle we're diving into today.

This isn't your average relationship roller coaster – it's more like a twisted version of "Groundhog Day" where the same patterns keep repeating, leaving you dizzy and disoriented.

The cycle typically goes something like this:

1. Idealization (aka The Honeymoon Phase): This is where the magic happens – or so it seems. Your narcissist is on their best behavior, showering you with attention, compliments, and promises. They're mirroring your interests, finishing your sentences, and making you feel like you've found your soulmate. It's intoxicating, right? But here's the catch: it's not real. They're creating an idealized version of themselves to hook you in.

2. Devaluation: Once they've got you firmly in their grasp, the true colors start to show. Suddenly, nothing you do is good enough. The person who once thought you hung the moon is now picking apart everything from your appearance to your achievements. It's subtle at first – a backhanded compliment here, a snide remark there. But over time, it escalates. You find yourself constantly walking on eggshells, trying to avoid their wrath and win back their approval.

3. Discard: This is where things get really painful. The narcissist might give you the silent treatment, openly flirt with others, or even leave you for someone else. They make you feel worthless and replaceable. But don't be fooled – the discard isn't always final. Often, it's just another act in their manipulative play, designed to keep you on an emotional rollercoaster.

4. Hoovering: Just when you think it's over and you're starting to pick up the pieces, they come swooping back in. Maybe they apologize, promise to change, or remind you of all the good

times. They might even play the victim, making you feel guilty for thinking of leaving. It's like they have a sixth sense for knowing exactly when you're about to break free.

And then? The cycle starts all over again. Rinse and repeat.

Now, you might be thinking, "If it's so bad, why don't people just leave?" Oh, if only it were that simple. See, this cycle is like quicksand – the more you struggle, the deeper you sink. It creates a trauma bond – a powerful emotional attachment that forms in abusive relationships. You become addicted to the highs of the idealization phase, always chasing that initial rush of love and validation.

Plus, the constant emotional upheaval messes with your brain chemistry. The highs and lows create a cocktail of hormones and neurotransmitters that can quite literally make you addicted to the relationship. It's not weakness – it's biology.

Understanding this cycle is the first step to breaking it. Once you can recognize these patterns, you start to see behind the curtain. That grand gesture isn't love – it's manipulation. The silent treatment isn't you being punished – it's them trying to regain control.

You didn't cause this cycle, you can't control it, and you certainly can't cure it. The only person who can break the cycle is you, by choosing to step off the merry-go-round.

In the next sections, we'll dive deeper into strategies for recognizing these patterns in real-time and, more importantly, how to extricate yourself from this toxic dance.

WHY IT'S SO HARD TO LEAVE A NARCISSISTIC PARTNER

Let's tackle the million-dollar question: Why is it so darn hard to leave a narcissistic partner? If you've been asking yourself this, you're not alone. And more importantly, you're not weak or stupid for staying. There are some powerful forces at play here.

Leaving a narcissist isn't like leaving a "normal" relationship. It's more like trying to escape a cult – complete with mind games, manipulation, and a whole lot of self-doubt. So cut yourself some slack, okay?

Now, let's break down why your brain might be keeping you stuck:

1. The Trauma Bond: Remember that cycle we talked about earlier? Well, it creates what psychologists call a trauma bond. It's like emotional superglue, binding you to your abuser through intense emotional experiences. Those highs and lows? They're addictive. Literally. Your brain gets hooked on the drama, making it incredibly hard to walk away.

2. Gaslighting Galore: After months or years of being told that you're "too sensitive" or "imagining things," you start to doubt your own reality. Maybe it's not so bad? Maybe it's all in your head? Let's set the record straight right now: it's not all in your head. Your experiences are real. Gaslighting is a powerful tool that can make you question everything you know to be true, but that doesn't make your perceptions any less valid.

3. The Sunk Cost Fallacy: You've invested so much time, energy, and love into this relationship. Walking away feels like admitting defeat. Your brain tricks you into thinking, "If I just try a little harder, it'll all be worth it." But here's a paradigm shift for you: it's not just okay to cut your losses – it's a brave and necessary step towards reclaiming your life. Investing in yourself isn't admitting defeat; it's choosing victory on your own terms.

4. Fear of the Unknown: Sure, your current situation might be miserable, but at least it's familiar. Leaving means stepping into the unknown, and that's scary as hell. Your brain prefers the devil it knows to the devil it doesn't.

5. Financial Entanglement: Narcissists love to create financial dependence. Maybe they control all the money, or perhaps you've built a life together that seems impossible to untangle. The prospect of starting over financially can be paralyzing.

6. The Children Factor: If you have kids, the stakes feel even higher. You might worry about the impact of divorce on them or fear losing custody to a manipulative ex. But remember, staying in an abusive relationship isn't doing your kids any favors either.

7. Societal Pressure: We live in a world that often prioritizes staying together over personal wellbeing. The fear of judgment from friends, family, or your community can be a powerful deterrent.

8. The Hoover Maneuver: Just when you're about to leave, they turn on the charm. Suddenly, they're the person you fell in love with

again. It's like they have a sixth sense for when you're slipping away, and they know exactly which buttons to push to reel you back in.

9. Rock Bottom Self-Esteem: After years of put-downs and manipulation, your self-esteem might be at rock bottom. You might feel like you don't deserve better or that no one else would want you. That's the narcissist talking, not reality.

10. Shame and Embarrassment: You might feel ashamed that you "let" this happen to you, or embarrassed to admit to others that your relationship isn't what it seems. Remember, abuse is never the victim's fault.

Understanding why it's hard to leave doesn't mean you have to stay. It means you can be kinder to yourself about why you've stayed so far, and it gives you the knowledge you need to start breaking those bonds.

Leaving a narcissist is like detoxing from a drug. It's hard, it's painful, and you might relapse a few times before you're free for good. On the other side of that pain is freedom, self-respect, and the chance to build a life filled with genuine love and respect.

You don't have to do this alone. There are people and resources out there to support you. And hey, you've already taken the first step by reading this and starting to understand what you're dealing with. That's huge!

CHAPTER 2

The Emotional Toll of Divorce from a Narcissist

COMMON EMOTIONAL EXPERIENCES

Let's talk about feelings. I know, I know – if you're anything like me, you might be tempted to skip this part. After all, haven't you been through enough already? But understanding the emotional rollercoaster you're on is crucial to getting off it. So buckle up, because we're about to dive into the wild world of post-narcissist emotions.

Whatever you're feeling right now? It's okay. Seriously. There's no "right" way to feel when you're divorcing a narcissist. Your emotions might be all over the place, and that's perfectly normal. Let's break down some of the common experiences:

1. Grief: Surprise! You might be mourning, even if you're the one who initiated the divorce. You're not just losing a partner; you're losing the dream of what your relationship could have been. That

fantasy of happily-ever-after? It's okay to grieve its loss. You might also be grieving the person you thought you were with – that charming, loving partner from the early days who turned out to be a mirage.

2. Anger: Oh boy, is this a big one. You might be angry at your ex for their manipulation and abuse. Angry at yourself for not seeing it sooner. Angry at the world for letting this happen. Guess what? That anger is valid. It's also a sign that you're starting to recognize your own worth. Just be careful not to let it consume you – we'll talk about healthy ways to express it later.

3. Fear: You might be afraid of being alone, of starting over, of what your ex might do. Financial fears, fears about your kids, fears about the future – they're all common and understandable. Remember, fear is a normal response to a big life change, but it doesn't have to control you.

4. Relief: You might also feel relief. Relief that the constant walking on eggshells is over. Relief that you don't have to pretend anymore. And you know what? It's okay to feel relieved. It doesn't negate the pain or mean the relationship wasn't important. It just means you're recognizing how heavy that burden was.

5. Confusion: Your brain might be a jumble of contradictory thoughts and feelings. One minute you're sure you're doing the right thing, the next you're second-guessing everything. This mental fog is a normal response to gaslighting and emotional abuse. It will clear with time and distance.

6. Guilt: Ah, the narcissist's favorite tool. You might feel guilty for "breaking up the family" or for "giving up." Remember, you didn't cause this situation. You're just refusing to enable it any longer.

7. Loneliness: Even if your relationship was toxic, you might feel intensely lonely after it ends. Humans are wired for connection, and the absence of even a bad relationship can leave a void. It's okay to feel lonely – it doesn't mean you made the wrong choice.

8. Hope: Yes, believe it or not, hope might start peeking through the clouds. Hope for a peaceful future, for genuine love, for the chance to rediscover yourself. Cherish these moments of hope – they're signposts pointing you toward your new life.

9. Numbness: Sometimes, you might not feel much of anything at all. Your emotional system has been through the wringer, and numbness can be its way of protecting you. It's okay if you're not feeling all the feels all the time.

10. Pride: As you start to break free, you might feel bursts of pride. Pride in your strength, in your courage to leave, in your resilience. Celebrate these moments – you've earned them!

The real twist in this emotional rollercoaster? You might feel all of these emotions in the span of a single day. Heck, you might feel them all in a single hour. It's like emotional whiplash, and it can leave you feeling drained and confused.

But remember, these feelings are all normal. They're your mind and heart processing a complex, traumatic experience. You're not crazy for feeling them. In fact, feeling them means you're human, and you're healing.

Think of these emotions like waves in the ocean. Sometimes they'll knock you off your feet. Other times, you'll ride them with grace. The key is to remember that, like waves, they'll come and go. No feeling, no matter how intense, lasts forever.

In the coming sections, we'll talk about healthy ways to cope with this emotional tsunami. We'll explore techniques for self-care, methods for processing your feelings, and strategies for rebuilding your emotional wellbeing.

For now, take a deep breath. Seriously, right now. Breathe in deeply, hold it for a count of four, and then let it out slowly. You've survived 100% of your worst days so far. You're stronger than you know, and you're not alone in this journey.

Healing isn't linear. You'll have good days and bad days. But each day, each breath, is a step forward. You're doing the hard work of reclaiming your life, and that's something to be proud of. So, be gentle with yourself. You're doing great, even when it doesn't feel like it.

DEALING WITH GASLIGHTING AND MANIPULATION DURING DIVORCE

Let's talk about one of the trickiest parts of divorcing a narcissist: dealing with their never-ending gaslighting and manipulation. Just when you think you're out, they pull you back in with their mind games. But don't worry, we're about to shine a light on their shadowy tactics.

Gaslighting is not just a buzzword. It's a serious form of emotional manipulation that makes you question your own reality. It's like someone's messing with the dimmer switch on your sanity. And during a divorce? They crank that sucker up to eleven.

Here's what gaslighting might look like during your divorce:

1. Rewriting History: Suddenly, your ex has a completely different recollection of your relationship. That time they screamed at you in public? "You're remembering it wrong. I never raised my voice." That agreement you made about the kids? "We never discussed that. You must be confused."

2. Playing the Victim: Watch out for the pity party. Your narcissistic ex might suddenly portray themselves as the wronged party. "How could you do this to me? After everything I've done for you?" They're trying to make you feel guilty for standing up for yourself.

3. Triangulation: This is when they bring other people into your conflict to support their version of reality. They might turn friends, family, or even your kids against you. "Everyone agrees with me. You're the one being unreasonable."

4. Moving the Goalposts: Just when you think you've reached an agreement, they change the terms. It's like playing football on a field where the end zone keeps moving. Exhausting, right?

5. Crazy-Making Behavior: They might deliberately provoke you and then accuse you of being "unstable" or "crazy" when you react. It's a classic set-up designed to make you look bad.

Now, here's the tricky part: dealing with this nonsense while trying to navigate a divorce can feel like trying to solve a Rubik's cube while riding a unicycle. Blindfolded. In a hurricane. But don't panic – here are some strategies to help you keep your footing:

1. Document Everything: And I mean everything. Every conversation, every agreement, every interaction. Emails, texts, voicemails – keep 'em all. This isn't just for legal purposes (though that's important too). It's also to help you maintain your grip on reality when they try to twist things.

2. Limit Direct Communication: The less contact you have, the fewer opportunities they have to mess with your head. Use email or a co-parenting app for necessary communication. Keep it brief, factual, and unemotional.

3. Build Your Support Team: Surround yourself with people who know your truth. A good therapist, trusted friends, a support group – these folks can help anchor you when you start to doubt yourself.

4. Practice the Grey Rock Method: When you have to interact, be as boring and non-reactive as possible. Think of yourself as a grey rock – uninteresting and unmovable. It's less fun for them if they can't get a rise out of you.

5. Trust Your Gut: You know what happened. You know your truth. When they try to make you doubt yourself, take a deep breath and remind yourself: "I know what I experienced."

6. Use the BIFF Response: When communicating, keep it Brief, Informative, Friendly, and Firm. Don't get drawn into emotional arguments or long explanations.

7. Focus on Self-Care: Gaslighting can take a serious toll on your mental health. Make sure you're taking care of yourself – eat well, get enough sleep, exercise, meditate. Your well-being is your best defense.

8. Educate Your Legal Team: Make sure your lawyer understands narcissistic personality disorder and the tactics your ex might use. A knowledgeable legal team can be your best ally in navigating this minefield.

Remember, the goal of gaslighting and manipulation is to keep you off-balance, to make you doubt yourself so you're easier to control. But you're onto them now. You see the game they're playing, and that knowledge is power.

It's not going to be easy. There might be days when you feel like you're losing your mind. But know that you're not. You're just dealing with someone who's an expert at twisting reality. Stay strong, stay focused, and keep reminding yourself of your truth.

You've already taken the hardest step by deciding to leave. Now it's about staying the course, even when the waters get choppy.

COPING WITH FEELINGS OF FAILURE OR SHAME

Let's talk about something you might not even want to admit to yourself: those pesky feelings of failure or shame. If you're nodding your head right now, thinking, "How did she know?", then take a deep breath. We're about to dive into this emotional minefield together.

First off, let me hit you with some real talk: feeling like you've failed or feeling ashamed about your divorce doesn't make you weak. It makes you human. And guess what? It's also completely normal when you're dealing with the aftermath of a narcissistic relationship.

Narcissists are experts at making everything your fault. They've probably spent years drilling it into your head that you're not good enough, that you're the problem, that if only you tried harder, loved more, or were better in some way, things would be perfect. And now that you're divorcing, those feelings might be hitting you like a ton of bricks.

But here's a powerful exercise to try right now. Stand tall, square your shoulders, and face yourself in the mirror. Now, with all the conviction you can muster, say these words out loud: "This is not my failure. This is not my shame to carry."

Let's break this down:

1. The Relationship Myth: We've all bought into this fairy tale that if we just find "the one," we'll live happily ever after. So when a relationship ends, especially a marriage, it can feel like a massive personal failure. But relationships are complex, and sometimes they just don't work out. That doesn't make you a failure. It

makes you someone brave enough to admit when something isn't working.

2. The Shame Game: Shame thrives in silence and secrecy. It wants you to believe you're alone in your experience, that no one else could possibly understand. But that's a big fat lie. So many others have walked this path before you, and they've not only survived but thrived.

3. The Perfectionism Trap: Maybe you're beating yourself up for not seeing the signs earlier, for staying too long, for "letting" yourself be manipulated. Cut it out, okay? You're not psychic, and hindsight is always 20/20. You did the best you could with the information you had at the time.

So, how do we start shifting these feelings? Here are some strategies:

1. Name it to Tame it: When you're feeling shame or like a failure, call it out. Say it out loud or write it down. "I'm feeling shame right now because..." Just naming the emotion can help reduce its power over you.

2. Practice Self-Compassion: Talk to yourself like you would a good friend. Would you tell your bestie they're a failure for leaving an abusive relationship? Heck no! So don't talk to yourself that way either.

3. Reframe Your Story: Instead of "I failed at my marriage," try "I was strong enough to leave a toxic situation." You're not a failure; you're a survivor.

4. Connect with Others: Remember how shame thrives in silence? Well, connection is its kryptonite. Reach out to supportive friends, join a support group, or consider therapy. Sharing your story can be incredibly healing.

5. Challenge Your Inner Critic: When that nasty voice in your head starts up with the "you're a failure" talk, challenge it. Ask for evidence. And guess what? That voice is usually full of hot air.

6. Educate Yourself: Learn about narcissistic abuse and its effects. Understanding what you've been through can help you see that your reactions and feelings are normal and valid.

7. Focus on Growth: Instead of dwelling on perceived failures, focus on what you've learned and how you've grown. This experience, as painful as it is, is shaping you into a stronger, wiser version of yourself.

Picture your healing journey as a winding mountain path rather than a straight highway. Some days you'll scale peaks of progress, feeling invincible. Other days, you might find yourself in valleys where old feelings of shame and failure cast long shadows. Both are natural parts of your ascent. Remember, every step forward counts, even if it doesn't always feel that way.

Every step you take away from shame and towards self-compassion is a victory.

RECOGNIZING AND CELEBRATING YOUR STRENGTH

Alright, superstar, it's time for a perspective shift. We've talked about the tough stuff, but now? Now the spotlight turns to something amazing: you. That's right, it's all about recognizing and celebrating your strength. And before you roll your eyes or think, "What strength? I'm a mess!" – hang on for a moment.

You know that saying, "You never know how strong you are until being strong is the only choice you have"? Well, guess what? You're living proof of that. You've been through the emotional equivalent of running a marathon while juggling flaming swords, and you're still here. That's not just strength – that's superhero-level resilience.

Let's break down some of the ways you've been kicking butt without even realizing it:

1. You Chose You: Making the decision to leave a narcissistic partner is like trying to escape quicksand. It takes enormous courage and strength to choose yourself, your sanity, and your future over the false comfort of a toxic relationship.

2. You're Facing Your Fears: Every day, you're confronting fears – fear of the unknown, fear of being alone, fear of what others might think. And yet, here you are, still moving forward. That's bravery in action, my friend.

3. You're Healing: Healing from narcissistic abuse is no walk in the park. It's more like climbing Everest in flip-flops. The fact that

you're doing this work, reading this book, seeking to understand and heal? That takes incredible strength and dedication.

4. You're Rewriting Your Story: You're in the process of reclaiming your narrative, of seeing through the gaslighting and manipulation to find your truth. That's not just strength – that's wisdom.

5. You're Surviving Day by Day: Some days, just getting out of bed and facing the world feels like a Herculean task. But you're doing it. Every day you keep going is a victory.

Now, you might be thinking. "But I don't feel strong. I cry, I doubt myself, I have bad days." Here's a secret: strength isn't about not having those moments. It's about having them and continuing anyway. It's about falling down seven times and getting up eight.

So, how do we start recognizing and celebrating this strength more? Glad you asked:

1. Keep a Victory Journal: Every day, write down one thing you did that took strength. It could be as simple as "I got out of bed" or as big as "I stood up for myself in court." Over time, you'll have a written record of your resilience.

2. Create a Strength Playlist: Curate a list of songs that make you feel powerful. Crank it up when you need a reminder of your inner warrior.

3. Practice Positive Self-Talk: Catch yourself when you're being

self-critical and flip the script. Instead of "I'm so stupid for staying so long," try "I'm so brave for leaving when I did."

4. Celebrate Small Wins: Did you set a boundary? Speak your truth? Navigate a difficult conversation with your ex? Celebrate it! Treat yourself to something special – you've earned it.

5. Surround Yourself with Cheerleaders: Spend time with people who recognize your strength and celebrate it. Their belief in you can help bolster your own.

6. Create a Strength Visual: Make a collage, vision board, or even just a list of words that represent your strength. Put it somewhere you'll see it every day.

7. Share Your Story: When you're ready, consider sharing your journey with others. Your story of resilience could be the inspiration someone else needs.

Remember, strength isn't about being invincible. It's about being broken and putting yourself back together, even if it's in a different shape than before. It's about facing your fears, owning your story, and choosing to keep going even when it's hard.

You, my friend, are a testament to the incredible resilience of the human spirit. You're not just surviving – you're on your way to thriving. And that's something worth celebrating.

CHAPTER 3

Protecting Your Mental Health

IMPORTANCE OF SELF-CARE DURING THIS TIME

The topic at hand is self-care. Now, before any eye-rolling begins at the thought of bubble baths and scented candles, let's set the record straight. This isn't about pampering; it's about fortifying mental health. And make no mistake, this isn't just important – it's the cornerstone of recovery and resilience.

Picture yourself on an airplane (remember those?), and the flight attendant is going through the safety instructions. What do they always say about oxygen masks? "Put your own mask on first before helping others." Well, consider this chapter your emotional oxygen mask.

Divorcing a narcissist is like running an emotional marathon while juggling chainsaws. It's intense, it's draining, and if you're not careful, it can leave you completely depleted. This is where self-care becomes your lifeline, your armor, your secret weapon. Forget any notions of it being selfish. In this battle, self-care isn't just important, it's do-or-die. Your well-being hangs in the balance, and the time to prioritize it is now.

Why is self-care a non-negotiable in this journey? Let's unpack the critical reasons:

1. Stress Management: Your stress levels are probably through the roof right now. Self-care helps you manage that stress before it manages you.

2. Emotional Resilience: Regular self-care builds up your emotional reserves, making you more resilient in the face of challenges.

3. Clarity of Thought: When you're taking care of yourself, you're better able to think clearly and make good decisions – something you need a lot of right now.

4. Physical Health: Mental stress can take a toll on your physical health. Self-care helps protect your body as well as your mind.

5. Setting Boundaries: Practicing self-care helps you get better at setting and maintaining boundaries – a crucial skill when dealing with a narcissist.

6. Modeling Healthy Behavior: If you have kids, you're showing them the importance of self-care and healthy coping mechanisms.

Now, I know what you're thinking. "I don't have time for self-care. I'm too busy dealing with lawyers/kids/work/life." I hear you. But here's the thing: you can't afford not to take care of yourself right now. It's like trying to drive a car without ever stopping for gas – eventually, you're going to break down.

So, what does real, effective self-care look like in the midst of divorce chaos? It's not about expensive spa days or tropical vacations (though if you can swing it, more power to you!). It's about small, consistent actions that nurture your mind, body, and soul. Here are some ideas to get you started:

1. Mindfulness and Meditation: Even five minutes a day can make a difference. Try apps like Headspace or Calm for guided meditations.

2. Physical Movement: Exercise is a powerful stress-buster. Whether it's a full workout, a walk around the block, or a dance party in your living room, get your body moving.

3. Sleep Hygiene: Prioritize your sleep. Create a bedtime routine, limit screen time before bed, and make your bedroom a peaceful sanctuary.

4. Healthy Eating: Nourish your body with good food. This isn't about strict diets – it's about fueling your body and mind with nutritious choices.

5. Creative Expression: Whether it's journaling, painting, singing, photography, knitting, or playing a musical instrument, find a creative outlet for your emotions.

6. Connection: Spend time with people who lift you up. Join a support group, call a friend, or connect with a therapist.

7. Nature Time: Spend time outdoors. Nature has a way of putting things in perspective and calming our nervous systems.

8. Saying No: Learn to say no to things that drain you. Your energy is precious right now – use it wisely.

9. Positive Self-Talk: Watch how you speak to yourself. Practice kind, encouraging self-talk.

10. Gratitude Practice: Even in tough times, there's always something to be grateful for. Try listing three things each day.

Self-care isn't one-size-fits-all. What works for your best friend might not work for you, and that's okay. The key is to find what resonates with you and make it a regular part of your routine.

Let's tackle the big, uncomfortable truth head-on: guilt. You might feel guilty for taking time for yourself when there's so much to do. But taking care of yourself isn't selfish – it's necessary. You can't pour from an empty cup, and you can't fight this battle if you're running on empty.

Let's make a pact right now. Think of one small thing you can do for yourself today. Maybe it's taking a 10-minute walk, calling a friend, or simply taking some deep breaths. Whatever it is, commit to doing it. You deserve it, and you need it.

Remember, you're not just going through a divorce – you're rebuilding your life. And that takes strength, energy, and resilience. By prioritizing self-care, you're giving yourself the tools you need to not just survive this process, but to come out the other side stronger and happier.

TECHNIQUES FOR MANAGING ANXIETY AND DEPRESSION

Alright, let's talk about those unwelcome guests called anxiety and depression. If you've been feeling like your mind is a pinball machine of worry or like you're stuck in a fog that just won't lift, you're not alone. Anxiety and depression are like the terrible twosome of divorce from a narcissist. But don't worry, we've got some tricks up our sleeve to help you show these uninvited guests the door.

It's totally normal to experience anxiety and depression during this time. You're not weak, you're not broken, and you're definitely not going crazy. You're human, and you're going through a tough time. Now, let's arm you with some tools to help you navigate these choppy emotional waters.

1. The Breath is Your Bestie: I know, I know, everyone tells you to "just breathe." But hear me out. Deep breathing actually changes your physiology and can calm your nervous system. Try this: breathe in for 4 counts, hold for 4, exhale for 4, hold for 4. Repeat this "box breathing" for a few minutes when anxiety strikes. It's like a chill pill without the pill.

2. Move That Body: Exercise isn't just for getting swole (though if that's your goal, go crush it!). It's a powerful weapon against both anxiety and depression. Even a 10-minute walk can boost your mood. Dance in your living room, do some yoga, tai chi or have a personal dance party. Your brain will thank you.

3. Mindfulness Isn't Just for Monks: Mindfulness is about being

present in the moment, and it can be a game-changer for anxiety. Try the 5-4-3-2-1 technique: Name 5 things you can see, 4 things you can touch, 3 things you can hear, 2 things you can smell, and 1 thing you can taste. Boom! You're back in the present.

4. Journaling: Not Just for Teenagers: Writing down your thoughts can help you process emotions and gain perspective. Don't worry about grammar or spelling - just let it flow. Bonus points if you end each entry with three things you're grateful for.

5. Cognitive Restructuring (Fancy Term for Thought Zapping): Anxiety and depression love to feed you lies. Challenge those thoughts! When you catch yourself thinking "I'll never be happy again," flip it to "This is temporary, and I will get through it." It takes practice, but it works.

6. Create a Worry Window: Set aside a specific time each day for worrying. Sounds weird, right? But giving yourself permission to worry for, say, 15 minutes a day can actually help you worry less overall. When worries pop up outside the window, tell them to come back during designated worry time.

7. Embrace the Power of 'No': Your well-being is paramount. Be selective about your commitments and interactions. It's okay to decline activities or relationships that drain you. Focus on what genuinely nurtures and fulfills you. Remember, saying 'no' to others often means saying 'yes' to yourself.

8. Connect with Your Tribe: Human connection is vital for healing.

Actively seek out supportive friends and family. Consider joining a support group where you can share experiences with others who understand. Don't underestimate the comfort that pets can provide - they offer unconditional love and can be great stress-relievers.

9. Sleep Isn't for the Weak: Prioritize your sleep. Create a bedtime routine, limit screen time before bed, and make your bedroom a sleep sanctuary. Good sleep is like kryptonite for anxiety and depression.

10. Seek Professional Guidance: There's no shame in seeking help from a therapist or counselor. They're like personal trainers for your mind. If you're struggling, reach out to a professional. It could be the best gift you give yourself.

Managing anxiety and depression isn't about being "cured" overnight. It's about building a toolkit of coping strategies and using them consistently. Some days will be better than others, and that's okay. The goal is progress, not perfection.

And here's a little secret: by working on managing your anxiety and depression, you're not just surviving this divorce - you're building skills that will serve you for the rest of your life. You're becoming more resilient, more self-aware, and more emotionally intelligent. In a weird way, your narcissistic ex is giving you the gift of personal growth. (Okay, maybe that's stretching it, but let's try to find the silver lining, shall we?)

DEALING WITH PTSD AND TRAUMA BONDING

Heads up, warrior - we're about to tackle some heavy hitters. PTSD and trauma bonding are often the unseen adversaries in the aftermath of narcissistic abuse. They're complex, they're challenging, but understanding them is crucial for your healing journey.

If you've been feeling like you're stuck in a time loop of bad memories or find yourself inexplicably missing your ex despite all the chaos, you're not going crazy. You're dealing with some serious psychological stuff, and we're going to break it down.

First up: PTSD, or Post-Traumatic Stress Disorder. Yeah, it's not just for war veterans. Surviving a relationship with a narcissist can leave you with some pretty intense battle scars too.

PTSD symptoms might look like:

- Flashbacks or nightmares about the relationship

- Feeling on edge all the time, like you're waiting for the other shoe to drop

- Avoiding people, places, or things that remind you of your ex

- Negative thoughts about yourself or the world

- Difficulty remembering parts of the relationship

Sound familiar? You're not alone, and more importantly, you're not weak. PTSD is your brain's way of trying to protect you from future harm. It's like your internal alarm system got stuck in the "on" position.

Now, let's talk about that other beast: trauma bonding. This is that frustrating phenomenon where you find yourself missing or longing for your ex, even though logically you know they were about as good for you as a chocolate-covered onion.

Trauma bonding happens because of the intense cycles of abuse followed by "love bombing" or periods of apparent kindness. It's like emotional whiplash, and it can create a powerful, addictive bond. Your brain gets hooked on the highs of the "good times," even though they're few and far between.

So, how do we start untangling this psychological knot? Here are some strategies:

1. Name It to Tame It: Recognizing that you're dealing with PTSD or trauma bonding is the first step. It's not "just in your head" - it's a real psychological response to trauma.

2. Grounding Techniques: When you feel a flashback coming on, try grounding yourself in the present. Use your senses - what can you see, hear, touch, smell, and taste right now?

3. Rewrite the Narrative: Challenge those rose-colored memories. When you find yourself missing your ex, remind yourself of the reality of the relationship. Keep a list of the negative experiences to read when you need a reality check.

4. Cut the Cord: No Contact (or as minimal contact as possible if you have kids) is crucial for breaking the trauma bond. Every interaction is like resetting the clock on your recovery.

5. Seek Professional Help: PTSD and trauma bonding are serious business. A therapist who specializes in trauma can be a game-changer in your recovery.

6. EMDR Therapy: Eye Movement Desensitization and Reprocessing (EMDR) therapy may be effective for processing traumatic memories.

7. Grow Your Support Network: Surround yourself with people who validate your experiences and support your healing. Consider joining a support group for survivors of narcissistic abuse.

8. Practice Self-Compassion: Be kind to yourself. Picture your healing journey as learning to surf. Some days you'll ride high on the waves; others, you might take a tumble. Both experiences make you a better surfer. Treat yourself like a supportive beach buddy – offer encouragement, celebrate the rides, and help yourself up after falls.

9. Create New, Positive Experiences: Start building new memories that have nothing to do with your ex. Take up a new hobby, travel, or volunteer. You're creating a new chapter in your life.

10. Educate Yourself: Understanding the psychology behind PTSD

and trauma bonding can help you feel more in control.

Healing from PTSD and breaking a trauma bond takes time. It's not about forgetting what happened - it's about processing it so it no longer controls you. You're rewiring your brain, and that's no small feat.

Here's the good news: every day you're healing, you're getting stronger. You're building resilience, self-awareness, and emotional intelligence that will serve you for the rest of your life. You're not just surviving - you're evolving into a more powerful version of yourself.

WHEN AND HOW TO SEEK PROFESSIONAL HELP

The mere thought of opening up to a stranger might make you want to crawl under a blanket and never come out. That's completely understandable. But understanding when and how to seek professional help could be the turning point you never knew you needed.

Let's face it, the idea of therapy can be intimidating. There's vulnerability, there's uncertainty, and maybe even a little skepticism. But consider this: just as you'd consult a doctor for a physical ailment, seeking help for emotional healing is equally valid and important.

There's absolutely no shame in asking for help. In fact, it's a sign of strength, not weakness. Think of it this way - if your car was making weird noises, you'd take it to a mechanic, right? Well, your mind is way more important than your car, so why not give it the same level of care?

So, when should you consider waving the white flag and calling in the pros? Here are some signs it might be time:

1. You're stuck in an emotional roundabout: If you feel like you're reliving the same painful emotions day after day with no improvement, it might be time for some professional guidance.

2. Your daily life is taking a hit: Are you struggling to get out of bed, missing work, or neglecting your relationships? That's a red flag, my friend.

3. You're turning to unhealthy coping mechanisms: If you find yourself reaching for the wine bottle a little too often or engaging in other destructive behaviors, it's time to call in backup.

4. You're having thoughts of self-harm: This is non-negotiable. If you're having thoughts of hurting yourself, please seek help immediately.

5. You're feeling isolated and alone: If you feel like no one in your life really gets what you're going through, a professional can offer that understanding and validation you're craving.

Now, let's talk about the "how" of seeking help. It can feel overwhelming, but rest assured, the process is often less daunting than it might seem at first glance.

1. Start with your primary care doctor: They can rule out any physical causes for your symptoms and refer you to mental health professionals.

2. Check your insurance: Many plans cover mental health services. Give them a call and ask about your coverage.

3. Employee Assistance Programs (EAP): If you're employed, check if your company offers an EAP. These often include free, confidential counseling sessions.

4. Online directories: Websites like *Psychology Today* have directories of therapists. You can filter by specialty, location, and insurance accepted.

5. Teletherapy options: Not ready to leave your house? No problem. Services like BetterHelp or Talkspace offer online therapy.

6. Support groups: Organizations like NAMI (National Alliance on Mental Illness) offer support groups that can be a great supplement to individual therapy.

7. Crisis hotlines: If you're in immediate distress, don't hesitate to call a crisis hotline. They're there 24/7 and can provide immediate support.

When you're ready to reach out, remember: you're interviewing them as much as they're assessing you. It's okay to shop around until you find a therapist you click with. Think of it like dating - sometimes you need to kiss a few frogs before you find your prince or princess of mental health.

And here's a pro tip: before your first session, jot down some notes about what you want to address. It's easy to get overwhelmed and forget important points once you're in the hot seat.

Seeking help isn't admitting defeat - it's arming yourself with new tools for the battle. It's like calling in air support when you've been fighting on the ground. You're not weak for needing help; you're smart for recognizing when you need to level up your game.

It's natural to feel apprehensive about this next step. However, remember that just beyond those fears lies a world of hope and healing. This journey may even lead you to rediscover aspects of yourself you thought were lost.

Consider this: you've already demonstrated incredible strength in surviving a narcissist. That same courage will undoubtedly see you through this next challenge.

Take a moment to breathe deeply and center yourself. You have the inner resources to face this. Imagine your future self looking back at this moment with pride and gratitude for the brave decision you're about to make.

CHAPTER 4

NAVIGATING THE LEGAL PROCESS

UNDERSTANDING YOUR RIGHTS

Brace yourself for a journey into the wild world of legal jargon and courtroom drama. It might feel like you're about to untangle a mile-long knot of holiday lights - frustrating and seemingly endless. Understanding your rights, however, is like having a secret weapon in your divorce arsenal.

Your rights are not just a catchy song by the Beastie Boys (though if you need a pump-up jam for your next court date, I highly recommend it). Your rights are the bedrock of your case, and knowing them inside and out can be the difference between getting steamrolled and standing your ground.

Navigating your rights during a divorce can feel like deciphering a complex legal puzzle. While the specifics can vary significantly based on your jurisdiction, there are some fundamental principles that generally apply. While this guide is here to help you understand the basics, consulting with a qualified divorce or family law attorney is the gold standard for truly understanding your specific rights and obligations.

1. The Right to a Fair Division of Assets: This isn't about who can hire the fanciest lawyer or who can shout the loudest. The law (in most places) says that marital assets should be divided equitably. Note that "equitable" doesn't always mean "equal" - it means fair.

2. The Right to Support: It's essential to be informed about your potential entitlements to spousal support, also known as alimony or maintenance in some jurisdictions. These financial provisions are governed by complex statutes that can vary significantly across different states or legal jurisdictions. Given the intricacies of family law, it's highly advisable to consult with a qualified family law attorney or a legal professional specializing in divorce proceedings. They can provide expert insights tailored to your specific situation and location, helping you navigate the nuanced landscape of spousal support laws. It's important to recognize that seeking financial support is a legitimate aspect of the divorce process. These provisions are designed to address economic imbalances that may arise from the dissolution of a marriage. Don't allow anyone, including your former partner, to discourage you from exploring your legal rights. Remember, understanding and pursuing what you're lawfully entitled to is not only your right but often a crucial step in ensuring your financial stability post-divorce. Approach this process with confidence, armed with professional legal advice and a clear understanding of your entitlements under the law.

3. The Right to Child Custody and Support: When children are involved in a divorce, their well-being becomes the paramount consideration in legal proceedings. As a parent, you have the right to pursue both custody arrangements and child support that serve the best interests of your children. In legal terms, "custody" often encompasses two distinct concepts: legal custody (decision-making authority for significant matters in the child's life) and physical custody (where the child primarily resides). Many jurisdictions now prefer terms like "parenting time" or "parental responsibilities" to reflect a more nuanced approach to post-divorce parenting arrangements. Child support, on the other hand, is typically calculated based on state-specific guidelines that consider factors such as each parent's income, the amount of parenting time, and the children's needs. It's crucial to approach these matters not from a perspective of "winning" or "losing," but rather with a focus on creating a stable, nurturing environment for your children. Courts generally favor arrangements that allow children to maintain meaningful relationships with both parents, unless circumstances dictate otherwise. Given the complexity and emotional nature of these issues, consulting with a family law attorney is highly advisable. They can provide guidance on your rights and help you navigate the legal process in a way that prioritizes your children's well-being. Remember, the goal is to establish a framework that supports your children's emotional, physical, and developmental needs in the post-divorce family structure.

4. The Right to a Safe Environment: If there's been any form of

abuse, you have the right to seek protection orders. Your safety (and your children's safety) comes first, always. Don't hesitate to document any incidents of threats or violence, as this evidence can be crucial in obtaining the legal protection you need.

5. The Right to Privacy: Your ex doesn't get carte blanche to dig through your personal life. There are limits to what can be demanded in discovery.

6. The Right to a Fair Hearing: The court is supposed to be an impartial referee. If you feel like you're not getting a fair shake, you have the right to speak up.

7. The Right to Appeal: If you think the court got it wrong, you generally have the right to appeal the decision.

Here's where it gets tricky. Narcissists have a nasty habit of trying to steamroll over your rights. They might try to intimidate you, manipulate you, or gaslight you into thinking you don't deserve what you're legally entitled to. Don't fall for it.

The more you understand about your rights, the less likely you are to be bullied or manipulated. So do your homework. Read up on your state's divorce laws. Talk to your lawyer (we'll get to choosing a good one in a bit). Join support groups for divorcing spouses - sometimes the best intel comes from those who've been in the trenches.

But here's a crucial point: knowing your rights is just the first step. The next step is standing up for them. And I know that can be scary, especially when you've been in a relationship where your voice was constantly silenced or dismissed. But you've got this. You're stronger than you know.

Think of it this way: every time you stand up for your rights, you're not just fighting for yourself. You're fighting for every person who's ever been bullied or manipulated by a narcissist. You're showing your kids (if you have them) what it looks like to demand respect and fair treatment. You're reclaiming your power, one legal right at a time.

So, are you ready to become a legal eagle? To transform from someone who feels powerless in the face of legalese to someone who can confidently assert their rights? It won't happen overnight, and there will probably be some bumps along the way. Each step forward, however, brings you closer to reclaiming your authentic self and the life you deserve.

In the next sections, we'll dive deeper into the nitty-gritty of the legal process. We'll talk about choosing the right lawyer, preparing for court, and dealing with your ex's legal shenanigans. But for now, take a deep breath, stand tall, and say: "I have rights, and I'm not afraid to fight for them."

Your resilience is your superpower. Let's show that courtroom who's boss.

CHOOSING THE RIGHT LAWYER

Let's talk about finding your legal soulmate. No, not that kind of soulmate (we'll get to dating post-divorce later). I'm talking about choosing the right lawyer. This decision is almost as important as choosing who to marry in the first place - and hopefully, you'll do a better job this time around!

Think of it this way: your lawyer is like your teammate in the most intense game of your life. You need someone who's not just good at the game, but who plays well with you. Someone who gets your style, understands your goals, and knows how to handle a narcissist's curveballs.

So, how do you find this legal unicorn? Let's break it down:

1. Seek Specialists: Look for lawyers who specialize in family law, and even better, those with experience dealing with high-conflict divorces or narcissistic personalities. You wouldn't go to a foot doctor for a heart problem, right? Same principle applies here.

2. Do Your Homework: Research potential lawyers like you're stalking an ex on social media (kidding... sort of). Check their websites, read reviews, look up their bar standing. Knowledge is power, people!

3. Interview Multiple Candidates: This isn't a one-and-done deal. Meet with at least three lawyers before making a decision. Many offer free consultations - take advantage of that!

4. Trust Your Gut: Pay attention to how you feel during the consultation. Do they listen to you? Do they explain things clearly? Or do they make you feel small and confused? Your lawyer should be your advocate, not another source of stress.

5. Discuss Strategy: Ask potential lawyers about their approach to cases like yours. Are they aggressive pit bulls or more collaborative negotiators? Make sure their style aligns with your goals.

6. Consider Your Budget: Let's be real - legal fees can add up faster than your ex's lies. Be upfront about your financial situation and understand their fee structure. Some lawyers offer payment plans or sliding scales.

7. Check Their Support Team: A great lawyer often comes with a great team. Ask about paralegals and assistants - they can be crucial in keeping your case (and costs) on track.

8. Assess Their Availability: Will you be able to reach them when you need to? Nothing's worse than feeling ghosted by your own lawyer.

9. Look for Red Flags: Beware of lawyers who make grand promises or guarantee outcomes. Divorce law is unpredictable, and an ethical lawyer will be upfront about that.

10. Consider Compatibility: You're going to be working closely with this person during one of the most stressful times of your life. Make sure you can communicate effectively and that you feel comfortable with them.

You're not just hiring a lawyer; you're building a partnership. This person is going to be privy to some of the most personal details of your life. They're going to be your voice in the courtroom. Make sure it's a voice you trust.

And here's a pro tip: if you're dealing with a narcissist, look for a lawyer who's familiar with high-conflict personalities. They should be able to anticipate your ex's tactics and have strategies to counteract them. Bonus points if they can explain these strategies to you without making you feel like you need a law degree to understand.

Now, I know what you're thinking. "This sounds like a lot of work. Can't I just pick the first name that pops up on Google?" Well, you could. But remember, this is your future we're talking about. Your financial security, your relationship with your kids, your peace of mind - it's all on the line. Isn't that worth a little extra effort?

When you do find that right fit, you'll know it. You'll feel more confident, more prepared, and ready to take on whatever your ex throws your way.

You're choosing an ally in your fight for freedom and fairness. Choose wisely, and let's show that narcissist what justice really looks like!

DOCUMENTING ABUSE AND GATHERING EVIDENCE

Alright, detective, it's time to put on your Sherlock Holmes hat. We're diving into the world of evidence gathering, and trust me, it's not as boring as it sounds. In fact, when you're dealing with a narcissist, documenting abuse and gathering evidence is like assembling the pieces of a puzzle that could finally show the world the true picture of what you've been dealing with.

Now, I know what you're thinking. "But I didn't take pictures of my bruises" or "It was all emotional abuse - how do I prove that?" Don't worry, we've got you covered. Emotional and psychological abuse might not leave visible scars, but that doesn't mean it can't be documented.

Let's break this down into manageable steps:

1. **Start a Journal:** This isn't your typical "Dear Diary" situation. We're talking about a detailed account of incidents, including dates, times, and exactly what was said or done. Be as specific as possible. "He was mean" doesn't cut it. "On June 15th at 7:30 pm, he called me stupid and worthless because I forgot to buy milk" - that's what we're looking for.

2. **Save Those Texts and Emails:** I know it's tempting to delete every nasty message, but resist the urge. Those digital footprints can be golden in court. Set up a separate folder or email account to store them if you need to.

3. **Voice Recordings:** Check your local laws first (some states require two-party consent), but if it's legal, consider recording verbal abuse. Your phone is a powerful tool - use it.

4. **Photographs and Videos:** If there's physical abuse or property damage, document it. Date-stamp those photos. And remember, a messy house after your ex trashed it in a rage is evidence too.

5. **Witness Statements:** Did anyone see or hear the abuse? Friends, family, neighbors, coworkers - their accounts can be valuable. Ask them to write down what they witnessed.

6. **Medical Records:** If you've sought medical attention due to abuse, those records are important evidence. This includes therapy for emotional abuse.

7. **Financial Records:** Financial abuse is real. Keep records of any

economic control or manipulation.

8. Social Media: Screenshots of threatening or abusive posts or messages can be powerful evidence. Don't forget to document their timestamp.

9. Police Reports: If you've ever called the police due to your ex's behavior, get copies of those reports.

10. Keep a Paper Trail: Any official documents related to your case - court orders, lawyer correspondence, etc. - keep them organized and accessible.

Now, here's the tricky part: gathering this evidence while staying safe. If you're still living with your abuser, be extra cautious. Use password-protected devices and accounts. Consider keeping your evidence in a safe place outside your home, like with a trusted friend or in a safety deposit box.

You're not just collecting this evidence for the court. You're also doing it for yourself. Gaslighting can make you doubt your own experiences. Having concrete evidence can help you stay grounded in reality and remind you that you're not crazy - you're dealing with a crazy situation.

But don't let evidence-gathering consume you. Yes, it's important, but so is your healing and moving forward. Set aside specific times for documentation, then allow yourself to focus on self-care and rebuilding your life.

And please, if you're in immediate danger, forget about evidence and focus on getting safe. No piece of evidence is worth your wellbeing or your life.

So, are you ready to become the Sherlock Holmes of your own life? To piece together the evidence that tells your true story? It might feel overwhelming at first, but remember: every text you save, every incident you document, is a step towards reclaiming your narrative and your power.

You've lived this story. Now it's time to tell it - with all the receipts to back it up. Let's show the world (and the court) the truth. You've got this, detective. Time to crack the case wide open!

DEALING WITH A NARCISSIST'S LEGAL TACTICS

Hold onto your sanity, because the courtroom circus is about to begin. If you thought your ex was a handful during your relationship, just wait until you see them in legal mode. It's like watching a toddler throw a tantrum, except this toddler has a law degree (or at least thinks they do).

But don't worry, we're going to arm you with the knowledge to see through their smoke and mirrors. Think of this as your personal guide to narcissist-proofing your divorce proceedings.

First up: The Delay and Deny Tactic

Imagine you're all set to move forward, and suddenly your ex needs more time. Or they conveniently "forget" to provide necessary documents. Or maybe they just flat-out deny agreeing to things you know you both discussed.

How to handle it: Document everything. I mean everything. Conversations, agreements, even that time they said they'd handle the car payment (and didn't). Keep a paper trail that would make an accountant jealous.

Next on the hit parade: The Financial Hide-and-Seek

Suddenly, your ex who bragged about their six-figure salary is crying poverty. Assets mysteriously disappear, or they claim that Rolex was "just a really good fake."

Your move: Work closely with your lawyer and possibly a forensic accountant. These financial Houdinis can often find money that your ex has squirreled away.

Let's not forget: The Smear Campaign

Your ex might try to paint you as unstable, unfit, or just plain crazy to anyone who'll listen - including the judge.

Your defense: Stay calm and let your actions speak louder than their words. Document any false allegations and stick to the facts. Remember, judges have seen it all before.

Ah, and the classic: The Courtroom Drama

Some narcissists love to turn the courtroom into their personal theater. They might cry on cue, play the victim, or try to charm the judge.

Your strategy: Don't get pulled into their performance. Stick to the facts, remain composed, and let your evidence do the talking.

And finally: The Settlement Seesaw

Just when you think you've reached an agreement, they back out or demand changes. It's like playing Monopoly with someone who keeps changing the rules.

How to deal: Set clear boundaries and stick to them. Don't let them wear you down with constant negotiations. Sometimes, letting a judge decide is less stressful than endless back-and-forth.

Now, here's the thing: dealing with these tactics can be exhausting. It's like playing chess with a pigeon - no matter how well you play, they'll knock over the pieces, poop on the board, and strut around like they've won.

But here's the secret: you win by not playing their game. Stay focused on your goals, not on "beating" them. Keep your cool, stick to the facts, and trust in the legal process.

Narcissists thrive on reaction and attention. By staying calm and businesslike, you're not giving them the emotional payoff they're looking for. It's like putting a toddler in time-out - eventually, they'll realize their tantrums aren't working.

On those days when it all feels too much? That's okay. Take a breather. Vent to a friend. Eat some ice cream. Self-care isn't just a buzzword - it's a survival strategy when you're dealing with a narcissist in court.

You've made it this far. You've survived their mind games, their manipulation, and their drama. This legal battle? It's just the final boss level. And guess what? You've got all the cheat codes right here.

So, are you ready to navigate this legal maze like a pro? To stand your ground and show that narcissist that their old tricks won't work anymore? Your strength is about to shine. And remember, every time you stand up to their tactics, you're not just fighting for yourself - you're showing others that it's possible to break free.

When it's showtime, let your authenticity be your strongest argument.

CHAPTER 5

Financial Survival and Recovery

Assessing Your Financial Situation

Alright, money mavens (or soon-to-be money mavens), it's time to talk about the green stuff. No, not kale smoothies (though they're great for stress-eating). We're diving into the world of finances post-narcissist. You'd probably rather get a root canal than look at your bank account right now. But this is the first step towards financial freedom, and it's not as scary as you think.

Let's start with assessing your financial situation. Think of it like taking inventory of your fridge after your roommate ate all your snacks. It might not be pretty, but you need to know what you're working with.

Remember, you're a survivor extraordinaire. You've weathered the storm of a narcissist's mind games - that's like emotional Olympics-level stuff. Compared to that, these financial figures? They're just a puzzle waiting for your brilliant mind to solve. You're more than equipped for this challenge.

Let's break it down:

1. The Grand Total: Make a list of all your assets. And I mean all of them. That collection of rare Beanie Babies? List it. Your great-aunt's china set? On the list it goes. Don't forget about retirement accounts, savings bonds, or that jar of loose change under your bed.

2. The Not-So-Grand Total: Time to face the music and list all your debts. Credit cards, mortgages, student loans, that $20 you owe your bestie for pizza - get it all down on paper. Knowledge is power, even when it's knowledge you'd rather not have.

3. Income Investigation: What's coming in each month? Include your salary, any alimony or child support, side hustles, even that $5 you found in your jeans pocket. Every little bit counts.

4. Expense Expedition: Track your spending for a month. And yes, that includes the $8 latte you grabbed this morning. No judgment here - we're just gathering intel.

5. Credit Check: Pull your credit report. It's like a financial report card, and you want to make sure your ex hasn't left any nasty surprises.

6. Future Forecast: Think about upcoming expenses. Will you need to move? Buy a car? Replace the laptop your ex "accidentally" spilled coffee on? List it out.

This might feel overwhelming. You might be staring at these numbers thinking, "How did I get here?" or "Will I ever recover from this?" But here's the thing: you're already on the path to recovery just by facing these numbers head-on.

Your financial situation right now is just that - your situation right now. It's not a life sentence. It's not a reflection of your worth. And it's certainly not the final chapter in your financial story.

You might be surprised by what you find. Maybe things aren't as bad as you feared. Or maybe they're worse. Either way, you now have a starting point. You can't map out a journey without knowing where you're beginning, right?

If you're looking at your list thinking, "I have no idea what half of this means," that's okay too. Financial literacy wasn't exactly taught in school (though it really should be). There's no shame in asking for help. A financial advisor, a trusted friend who's good with money, or even some good old-fashioned Google Fu can help you make sense of it all.

The most important thing? Don't judge yourself. Your ex may have controlled the finances, or maybe money was a source of conflict in your relationship. Whatever the case, you're taking control now, and that's what matters.

Alright, money mavericks, are you prepared to tackle those figures? To take that first step towards financial independence? It might not be a thrill ride, but it's the beginning of something amazing - your financial comeback story.

Grab a cup of coffee (or a glass of wine - no judgment here), put on your favorite empowering playlist, and let's dive in. Your resilience has already conquered mountains - these spreadsheets are just molehills in comparison. Time to flex those financial muscles!

PROTECTING YOUR ASSETS DURING DIVORCE

Alright, financial ninjas, it's time to talk about protecting your assets during divorce. And no, I don't mean stuffing cash under your mattress or burying gold in the backyard (though I won't judge if you've considered it). We're talking about smart, legal ways to ensure you don't get the short end of the financial stick in your divorce.

Think of this as your personal asset protection boot camp. By the end of this section, you'll be ready to guard your finances like a mama bear protects her cubs. Let's dive in!

1. Knowledge is Power: Know what you've got. Remember that financial inventory we did? That's your secret weapon. Make copies of all important financial documents: bank statements, tax returns, investment accounts, retirement plans, the works. If it's got a dollar sign on it, you want a copy.

2. Separate and Conquer: If you haven't already, open your own bank account and credit card. It's time for financial independence, baby! Make sure your paycheck is going into your account, not a joint one.

3. Change Those Passwords: If your ex knows your online banking

password, it's time for an upgrade. And no, your dog's name followed by '123' doesn't count as secure. Get creative!

4. Freeze Joint Accounts: If you have joint accounts, consider freezing them so neither of you can make withdrawals without the other's consent. It's like putting your shared piggy bank in time-out.

5. Track Joint Expenses: If you're still using joint accounts for household expenses, keep meticulous records. You don't want to be on the hook for your ex's sudden passion for collecting rare tropical fish.

6. Beware of Revenge Spending: Some spouses go on spending sprees when divorce is on the horizon. If you notice unusual activity, alert your lawyer pronto.

7. Don't Make Any Big Money Moves: Now's not the time to buy that sports car you've always wanted or invest in your cousin's llama farm. Major financial decisions can complicate your divorce proceedings.

8. Get Appraisals: That antique vase your ex claims is worthless? Get it appraised. Same goes for the house, the car, and yes, even the wedding china you never use.

9. Explore the Possibility of a Postnuptial Agreement: If divorce isn't on the immediate horizon but you're concerned about protecting your assets, it might be worth discussing a postnuptial

agreement with a lawyer. However, it's crucial to understand that the enforceability of postnuptial agreements varies significantly depending on your location. Some states recognize and enforce these agreements, while others may view them with skepticism or not recognize them at all. Your local laws and specific circumstances will play a big role in determining whether this is a viable option for you. A consultation with a family law attorney familiar with your state's laws can provide clarity on whether a postnuptial agreement could be a useful tool in your situation.

10. Be Wary of "Sudden Business Failure": If your spouse owns a business and suddenly claims it's failing, put on your detective hat. Some sneaky spouses try to hide assets by understating business value.

11. Watch Out for Hidden Assets: Keep an eye out for suspicious behavior like unusual cash withdrawals, mysterious new P.O. boxes, or sudden "gifts" to family members.

12. Protect Your Inheritance: If you've received an inheritance, make sure it's in a separate account under your name only. Don't commingle it with marital funds.

13. Consider a Trust: In some cases, setting up a trust can help protect certain assets. Talk to a financial advisor or lawyer about whether this is right for you.

14. Don't Forget Digital Assets: Cryptocurrencies, online businesses, even valuable domain names - make sure these are accounted for

in your asset division.

15. Keep Your Cool: I know it's tempting to set fire to your ex's designer shoe collection, but resist the urge. Destroying or hiding assets can get you in big trouble with the court.

The goal here isn't to "hide" assets or pull a fast one on your ex. That's their game, not yours. You're aiming for fair protection of what's rightfully yours.

And here's a pro tip: document, document, document. If you make any financial moves during this time, keep records and be prepared to explain your actions. Transparency is your friend.

This might feel a bit like preparing for financial warfare. But think of it as building a fortress around your future. Every step you take to protect your assets is a step towards financial independence and stability.

You've already shown incredible strength by leaving a narcissist. Now it's time to show that same strength in protecting your financial future.

So, are you ready to become a financial protection pro? To stand guard over your assets like a dragon guarding its treasure? It's time to transform your fiscal finesse into an impenetrable fortress.

CREATING A POST-DIVORCE BUDGET

Alright, budget bosses-in-training, it's time to talk about everyone's favorite topic: budgeting! Cue the imaginary eye rolls and exasperated sighs. But hang tight, because creating a post-divorce budget isn't just about pinching pennies – it's about constructing your fiscal fortress, one well-placed dollar at a time.

Think of your new budget as your financial GPS. It's not there to scold you for buying that latte (though maybe reconsider if it's your fifth one today). It's there to guide you towards your goals and help you avoid those pesky financial potholes along the way.

So, let's break this down into bite-sized, non-scary chunks:

1. Start with Your Income: List out all your sources of income. Salary, alimony, child support, side hustle money from selling your ex's baseball card collection (kidding, don't do that). This is your starting point.

2. Essential Expenses: These are your "must-haves." Rent/mortgage, utilities, groceries, insurance, debt payments. You know, the stuff that keeps a roof over your head and keeps the lights on.

3. Savings and Emergency Fund: Yes, I'm putting this before fun stuff. Why? Because Future You will thank Present You for this foresight. Even if it's just a small amount, start building that safety net.

4. Transportation Costs: Whether it's a car payment, public transit pass, or just keeping your bicycle in tip-top shape, factor in how you're getting from A to B.

5. Health and Wellness: This includes medical expenses, gym memberships, and yes, maybe that yoga class that keeps you sane.

Your mental health is just as important as your financial health.

6. Personal Spending: This is your "fun money." Eating out, entertainment, hobbies. It's important to include this – a budget that's all work and no play makes for a very dull (and unsustainable) financial life.

7. Kids' Expenses (if applicable): School supplies, activities, clothes they outgrow every 5 minutes. Kids are wonderful, but let's face it, they're not cheap.

8. Debt Repayment: If you've got debts, make a plan to tackle them. Even small extra payments can make a big difference over time.

9. Professional Development: Investing in yourself is always a good move. This could be classes, certifications, or networking events to boost your career.

10. Miscellaneous: There's always something that doesn't fit neatly into a category. Give yourself a little wiggle room for life's surprises.

Be realistic. If you try to cut out every single "extra" expense, you're setting yourself up for failure. It's like going on a crash diet – you might stick to it for a while, but eventually, you'll find yourself elbow-deep in a pint of ice cream wondering what went wrong.

Instead, aim for balance. Maybe you can't afford weekly manicures anymore, but can you do an at-home spa night once a month? It's about finding creative ways to live well within your means.

Your budget is a living document. As your life changes, your budget should too. Got a raise? Awesome, adjust accordingly. Unexpected expense? Take a deep breath and tweak your numbers.

Here's a pro tip: use the 50/30/20 rule as a starting point. That's 50% of your income for needs, 30% for wants, and 20% for savings and debt repayment. It's not set in stone, but it's a good framework to begin with.

Now, looking at these numbers might make you feel a bit...well, number. But you're not just creating a budget. You're creating a roadmap to your new life. Every dollar you allocate is a step towards independence, security, and yes, even happiness.

So, are you ready to become the boss of your own budget? To take control of your finances and show your ex (and the world) that you've got this? Grab your calculator (or your phone's calculator app, let's be real), pour yourself a beverage of choice, and let's crunch some numbers. Your financial future is waiting, and it looks pretty darn bright from here.

REBUILDING YOUR FINANCIAL LIFE

Financial phoenixes, the time has come to spread those wings and soar into a new era of fiscal empowerment! The prospect of rebuilding might seem daunting, perhaps even tempting you to burrow under the covers and hibernate. But resist that urge, because this is where the journey takes an exhilarating turn. This isn't about merely patching up the old; it's about crafting a gleaming new financial blueprint for a fabulous future.

Picture this as the grand opening of "You, Inc." - a fresh start where you're the CEO, CFO, and visionary all rolled into one. The slate is clean, the possibilities endless, and the potential for growth? Skyscraper-high. So, grab that metaphorical hard hat and those blueprints. It's time to construct a financial fortress that's not just sturdy, but spectacular.

Let's dive into the steps to rebuild your financial life:

1. Set Clear Goals: What do you want your financial future to look like? Maybe it's owning a home, starting a business, or just having enough savings to sleep peacefully at night. Write these goals down - there's power in putting pen to paper. To make your goals more achievable, use the SMART criteria: make them Specific, Measurable, Achievable, Relevant, and Time-bound. For example, instead of "save more money," try "save $10,000 for a home down payment in the next 18 months." This approach not only clarifies your objectives but also provides a roadmap for action, making it easier to track your progress and stay motivated as you work towards your financial dreams.

2. Boost Your Financial Literacy: Knowledge is power, especially when it comes to money. Read books, listen to podcasts, take a class. Become the financial wizard you were always meant to be. Consider joining online communities or local groups focused on financial education, where you can share experiences, learn from others, and stay motivated on your financial journey. Remember, financial literacy isn't just about understanding complex terms or mastering investment strategies; it's about gaining the confidence to make informed decisions, ask the right questions, and take control of your financial future – skills that will serve you well in all aspects of life, from negotiating a raise to teaching your

children about money management.

3. **Rebuild Your Credit:** Your credit score might have taken a hit during your marriage or divorce. Time to nurse it back to health. Pay bills on time, keep credit card balances low, and consider a secured credit card if needed. Regularly monitor your credit report for errors or signs of identity theft, and dispute any inaccuracies promptly – you're entitled to a free credit report from each of the three major credit bureaus annually. Remember, rebuilding credit is a marathon, not a sprint; it may take several months or even a couple of years to see significant improvements, but consistent responsible financial behavior will gradually boost your score, opening doors to better interest rates and financial opportunities in the future.

4. **Diversify Your Income:** Don't put all your eggs in one basket. Consider a side hustle, freelance gig, or passive income stream. Who knows, your divorce might just be the push you needed to start that Etsy shop selling snarky cross-stitch patterns. Exploring multiple income streams not only provides financial stability but can also be a fantastic way to rediscover old passions, develop new skills, and build a network outside your primary career. Remember, the goal isn't necessarily to work more hours, but to make your existing skills and interests work harder for you – whether it's tutoring in a subject you love, monetizing a hobby, or investing in dividend-paying stocks.

5. **Invest in Yourself:** Your greatest asset is you. Consider additional

education or training to boost your earning potential. Maybe it's time to finally get that certification or degree you've been dreaming about. Remember that investing in your skills and knowledge not only increases your market value but also boosts your confidence, opens up new career opportunities, and can provide a sense of personal fulfillment that extends far beyond the workplace. Moreover, in today's rapidly changing job market, continuous learning isn't just an option—it's a necessity to stay competitive and adaptable, so view your personal development as a lifelong journey rather than a one-time effort.

6. Build Your Emergency Fund: Aim to set aside 3-6 months of living expenses in a readily accessible savings account. This financial cushion serves as a crucial safety net, providing peace of mind and stability during unexpected life events. Start by calculating your essential monthly expenses, including rent/mortgage, utilities, food, and healthcare costs. Then, gradually work towards saving this amount, even if it means starting with small, consistent contributions. An emergency fund acts as a buffer against job loss, medical emergencies, or unforeseen major expenses, preventing the need to rely on high-interest credit cards or loans in times of crisis. Moreover, having this financial security can empower you to make better long-term decisions, knowing you have a solid foundation to fall back on.

7. Start Investing, But Do It Wisely: The power of investing, especially when harnessed early, can seem magical thanks to

compound interest. However, it's crucial to approach investing with caution and knowledge. Before diving in, strongly consider seeking advice from a qualified financial advisor and do your due diligence. Never invest money you can't afford to lose, and be prepared for market fluctuations. Start small if you're unsure.

8. Reassess Your Insurance Needs: Life changes mean insurance needs change too. Make sure you're adequately covered without overpaying. This includes reviewing your health, life, disability, homeowners or renters, and auto insurance policies to ensure they align with your current circumstances and future goals. Consider consulting with an independent insurance broker who can compare policies from multiple providers, potentially helping you find better coverage at more competitive rates, and remember to review your insurance needs annually or after any significant life event such as marriage, divorce, birth of a child, or career change.

9. Plan for Retirement: It might seem far off, but Future You will be incredibly grateful if you start planning now. Consider maxing out that 401(k) if you can, as this not only builds your nest egg but often comes with valuable employer matching contributions. If a 401(k) isn't available or you've maxed it out, explore other retirement savings vehicles like Individual Retirement Accounts (IRAs), which offer tax advantages and a wide range of investment options to suit your long-term financial goals.

10. Create a Will and Estate Plan: Not the most fun topic, but it's important. Make sure your assets are protected and your wishes

are clear. This is especially crucial if you have children, as a will allows you to name guardians and ensure your kids are cared for according to your preferences. Moreover, a comprehensive estate plan can help minimize taxes, avoid lengthy probate processes, and prevent potential family disputes, ultimately providing peace of mind for you and your loved ones.

11. Seek Professional Help: Consider working with a financial advisor. They can help you create a personalized plan to reach your goals. When selecting an advisor, look for credentials such as Certified Financial Planner (CFP) or Chartered Financial Analyst (CFA), and ensure they are fiduciaries who are legally obligated to act in your best interest. Remember, a good financial advisor should not only help with investment strategies but also assist with comprehensive financial planning, including tax optimization, estate planning, and risk management tailored to your unique situation.

12. Celebrate Small Wins: Did you stick to your budget this month? Boost your credit score by 10 points? Time for a victory dance! Who cares if you look like a caffeinated octopus having a seizure? You're financially winning, and that's what matters! Acknowledging progress keeps you motivated, so don't be shy about celebrating those fiscal victories. Resisted the urge to buy those designer shoes? Treat yourself to a goofy happy dance. Finally figured out what APR stands for without Googling? You've earned the right to wear your "Financial Wizard" hat for the day. Remember, personal finance doesn't have to be all stern

faces and spreadsheets. A little fun can make money management less daunting and more rewarding. So go ahead, do your happy money dance – your bank account is silently cheering you on!

Rebuilding your financial life is a journey, not a destination. There will be ups and downs, and that's okay. The important thing is that you're taking control and moving forward.

And here's a little secret: this process can actually be... fun. (I know, I was surprised too!) There's something incredibly empowering about taking charge of your finances. Each step you take is a move towards independence and security.

RESOURCES FOR FINANCIAL ASSISTANCE

Alright, treasure hunters, it's time to uncover the hidden gems of financial assistance! I know what you're thinking: "Financial assistance? Sounds about as exciting as watching paint dry." But stick with me, because we're about to dive into a world of resources that could be total game-changers for your post-divorce life.

Think of this section as your personal financial treasure map. We're not talking about digging for buried gold here (though if you find some, let me know). We're talking about real, practical resources that can help you get back on your feet and even give you a leg up in your new life.

So, let's explore the bounty of financial assistance out there:

1. Government Programs: Uncle Sam might not be your favorite relative right now, but he's got some tricks up his sleeve:

- Temporary Assistance for Needy Families (TANF)
- Supplemental Nutrition Assistance Program (SNAP)
- Low Income Home Energy Assistance Program (LIHEAP)
  Don't let pride stop you from exploring these options. You've paid taxes; it's okay to use the system when you need it.

2. Non-Profit Organizations: There are angels among us, and some of them run non-profits:

   - Women's shelters often offer financial counseling and assistance
   - Local churches and community centers may have support programs
   - The YWCA offers various programs for women in transition

3. Legal Aid: Drowning in legal fees? There's hope:

   - Legal Aid societies offer free or low-cost legal services
   - Many bar associations have pro bono programs
   - Some law schools run clinics where students (supervised by attorneys) can help

4. Credit Counseling: Get your credit back on track:

   - The National Foundation for Credit Counseling offers free or low-cost counseling

- Many credit unions provide financial counseling to members

5. Housing Assistance: Need a roof over your head?

    - Check out the Housing Choice Voucher Program (Section 8)
    - Look into local rent assistance programs
    - Habitat for Humanity might be an option if you're looking to own

6. Education and Career Resources: Time to level up your skills:

    - The Workforce Innovation and Opportunity Act offers training programs
    - Many community colleges have programs for displaced homemakers
    - Check out grants specifically for single parents returning to school

7. Healthcare: Because your health matters:

    - Look into Medicaid or the Children's Health Insurance Program (CHIP)
    - Many hospitals have financial assistance programs
    - Don't forget about mental health resources - many offer sliding scale fees

8. Food Banks and Meal Programs: Keep yourself and your kids well-fed:

    - Local food banks can be a huge help

    - Schools often have free or reduced lunch programs

    - Meals on Wheels isn't just for seniors - some programs help families too

9. Childcare Assistance: Because little ones are expensive:

    - The Child Care and Development Fund offers assistance to low-income families

    - Head Start and Early Head Start programs provide free preschool

    - Some YMCAs offer affordable childcare options

10. Financial Education: Knowledge is power (and money):

    - Many banks offer free financial literacy workshops

    - Check out online resources like Khan Academy for free financial education

    - Your local library might offer financial planning classes

Using these resources isn't a sign of weakness - it's a smart strategy for getting back on your feet. Think of it as assembling your own personal financial Avengers team. Each resource is a superhero with its own special power to help you conquer your financial challenges.

Don't be afraid to ask for help. Reach out to local organizations, explain your situation, and see what they can offer. You might be surprised at the support that's available when you start looking.

So, are you ready to start your treasure hunt? To uncover the financial assistance that could make your transition smoother and your future brighter? Grab your metaphorical map and compass, and let's start exploring. There's a world of support out there waiting for you, and you deserve every bit of it.

Every step you take towards financial stability is a step away from your past and towards your amazing new future. Now you've got an arsenal of resources to help you along the way. Let's turn those financial lemons into the sweetest lemonade you've ever tasted!

CHAPTER 6

Co-Parenting with a Narcissist

PROTECTING YOUR CHILDREN FROM NARCISSISTIC ABUSE

Alright, super parents, it's time to shine a spotlight on the trickiest part of your post-divorce adventure - navigating the co-parenting minefield with your narcissistic ex. Buckle up, because we're about to dive into the wild world of protecting your kiddos from narcissistic abuse while maintaining your sanity. It's like trying to navigate a minefield while juggling flaming torches, but take heart! This guide is here to light the way and help you find safe passage.

Let's start with the most important thing: You are your child's superhero. You might not wear a cape (or maybe you do, no judgment here), but you're the shield between your little ones and the chaos of narcissistic behavior. So let's suit up and get to work!

Protecting your children from narcissistic abuse is like being a secret agent. Your mission, should you choose to accept it (who are we kidding, of course you accept it), is to create a safe, loving environment for your kids while dealing with a co-parent who's... let's say, challenging.

Here's your spy kit for this mission:

1. Be the Emotional Anchor: Your ex might be an emotional rollercoaster, but you can be the steady ground. Provide consistency, love, and emotional stability. Be the parent your kids can always count on.

2. Communicate Clearly and Directly with Your Kids: Explain things in age-appropriate ways. Don't badmouth your ex (tempting as it might be), but do validate your children's feelings. "It's okay to feel upset when Dad breaks promises" is much better than "Your father is a lying jerk" (even if it's true).

3. Set Clear Boundaries: Establish rules and routines in your home. This gives kids a sense of security and helps counteract the chaos they might experience with your ex.

4. Document Everything: Keep a record of interactions, incidents, and concerns. It's like your co-parenting diary, but less "Dear Diary" and more "Exhibit A."

5. Use the Grey Rock Method: When dealing with your ex, be as boring as possible. Respond to attempts at drama or manipulation with the enthusiasm of, well, a grey rock. It's not exciting, but it's effective.

6. Teach Your Kids About Healthy Relationships: Show them what respect, kindness, and healthy boundaries look like. You're their best role model for normal, loving relationships.

7. Encourage Open Communication: Create a safe space for your kids to express their feelings without fear of judgment. Be their emotional safe haven.

8. Protect Their Privacy: Don't use your kids as messengers or spies. They're not your little secret agents in your ex's camp.

9. Seek Professional Help: A child therapist can be a great neutral party to help your kids process their feelings and experiences.

10. Take Care of Yourself: Nurturing yourself isn't a luxury, it's a necessity. When you recharge your own batteries, you're better equipped to power through parenting challenges. Remember, a thriving parent is the best gift you can give your kids.

You're playing the long game here. Your ex might win some battles (like being the "fun" parent who doesn't enforce bedtime), but you're winning the war by providing stability, love, and emotional health.

And here's a nugget of wisdom: Your children are incredibly perceptive. They'll gradually piece together the reality of the situation. Your mission is to be their safe harbor when that realization hits. Be ready with open arms, a listening ear, and perhaps a comfort-food feast of their choosing - whether it's homemade cookies or a build-your-own sundae bar.

It's not going to be easy. There will be days when you want to scream into a pillow or hide in the closet with a giant bag of chocolate (been there, done that). But you've got this. You're stronger than you know, and your kids are lucky to have you in their corner.

So, are you ready to be the superhero your kids need? To navigate the treacherous waters of co-parenting with a narcissist like the boss you are? Grab your invisible shield (and maybe some wine for later), and let's do this. Your kids are counting on you, and trust me, you're more than up for the challenge.

In the story of your kids' lives, you're not just a character - you're the author of their happily ever after. Now, let's write a bestseller, shall we?

ESTABLISHING BOUNDARIES IN CO-PARENTING

You might be thinking. "Easier said than done!" And you're right – setting boundaries with a narcissist isn't exactly a walk in the park. Don't sweat it, think of this book as your personal strategy coach. Let's break down some practical ways to flex those boundary-setting muscles:

1. The Non-Negotiables List: Time to channel your inner diva and make a list of your absolute must-haves. No name-calling in front of the kids? Check. Sticking to agreed schedules? Double-check. Think of it as your co-parenting constitution.

2. Become a Communication Ninja: When it comes to talking with your ex, think "short and sweet" – minus the sweet part. Stick to the facts, keep it child-focused, and resist the urge to

write a novel-length response to every message. Remember, you're aiming for "cool cucumber," not "spicy jalapeño."

3. Embrace Your Inner Gray Rock: No, I'm not suggesting you turn into actual stone (though sometimes that might seem appealing). The "Gray Rock" method is all about being as boring and unreactive as possible. Think of yourself as the world's dullest documentarian – just the facts, no drama.

4. Get It in Writing: A detailed parenting plan is your new best friend. It's like a GPS for your co-parenting journey – when you feel lost, it'll help you find your way back to the right path.

5. There's an App for That: Co-parenting apps are like the Switzerland of divorced parents – neutral territory for all your communication needs. Plus, they keep records. Because sometimes, you need receipts.

6. Master the Art of Emotional Bubble Wrap: Imagine wrapping your heart and mind in bubble wrap. Your ex's words and actions can't pop your bubbles if you don't let them. It takes practice, but it's oh-so-worth it.

7. Be a Boundary Bodyguard: Once you set those boundaries, guard them like they're the last slice of pizza. Be consistent, follow through, and don't let those sneaky boundary-crossing attempts slide.

8. Teach Your Kids the Boundary Boogie: Help your kiddos learn

the boundary dance too. It's a life skill that'll serve them well, whether they're dealing with their other parent or that kid at school who always tries to steal their lunch.

Setting boundaries isn't about being mean or difficult. It's about creating a healthier, more peaceful environment for you and your kids. It's about reclaiming your power and your sanity in a situation that can often feel overwhelming.

Will it be easy? Probably not. Will there be days when you want to throw in the towel and move to a deserted island? Most likely. But you're stronger than you know. You've already survived a divorce from a narcissist, for crying out loud! You're practically a superhero.

So, take a deep breath, straighten that invisible cape, and get ready to rock those boundaries. You've got this, and I'm right here cheering you on. After all, we boundary-setting parents have to stick together!

DEALING WITH PARENTAL ALIENATION

Picture this: You're excited to pick up your kids for your weekend together. You've got a fun-filled couple of days planned - maybe some board games, a trip to the park, and their favorite homemade pizza. But when you arrive, you're met with cold shoulders, eye rolls, and mumbled "do we have to go?"s. Ouch. What gives?

Welcome to the twisted world of parental alienation, folks. It's like your ex has suddenly morphed into the evil queen from Snow White, offering your kids a shiny red apple of lies and manipulation. And let me tell you, it's enough to make even the most zen parent want to pull their hair out.

But before you go all Rapunzel on us, let's take a deep breath and dive into what's really going on here. Because knowledge is power, my friends, and we're about to arm you with a whole arsenal of it.

So, what's the deal with parental alienation? In a nutshell, it's when one parent systematically badmouths, belittles, or manipulates the kids against the other parent. It's like they're rewriting your family's story, and suddenly you're the big bad wolf instead of the loving parent you know you are.

Signs your ex might be playing the alienation game include:

1. Your kids suddenly become critical or dismissive of you for no apparent reason.

2. They use adult language or parrot your ex's negative views about you.

3. Your children refuse to spend time with you or your extended family.

4. They show unwavering support for your ex, even when they're clearly in the wrong.

5. Your kids have detailed knowledge of adult issues, like your divorce proceedings.

If you're nodding your head so hard it might fall off, don't worry. You're not alone, and more importantly, you're not powerless.

Now, your first instinct might be to go all mama or papa bear and fight fire with fire. But trust me, getting into a "who can trash-talk the other parent better" competition is about as productive as trying to nail jello to a wall. Instead, let's look at some strategies that actually work:

1. Keep Your Cool, Captain: I know, easier said than done. But reacting with anger or frustration only proves your ex right in your kids' eyes. Instead, be the calm in the storm. Show them that no matter what, you're a safe harbor.

2. Be the Bigger Person (Yes, Even When It Sucks): Never, ever badmouth your ex to your kids. I know, sometimes it feels like they're practically begging you to join the mud-slinging contest. Don't take the bait. Your high road might feel lonely now, but it'll pay off in the long run.

3. Document, Document, Document: Channel your inner Sherlock Holmes and keep detailed records of alienating behaviors. Times, dates, what was said or done. It might come in handy if you need to take legal action.

4. Quality Over Quantity: Make the time you have with your kids count. Create positive experiences and memories that contradict the negative narrative they're being fed.

5. Open Those Communication Lines: Keep talking to your kids, even when it feels like you're talking to a brick wall. Let them know you're always there to listen, without judgment.

6. Seek Professional Backup: A family therapist can be your secret

weapon in this battle. They can help your kids process their feelings and see through the manipulation.

7. Know When to Seek Legal Help: If the alienation is severe and persistent, it might be time to talk to your lawyer about modifying custody arrangements.

Dealing with parental alienation is tough, no two ways about it. There might be days when you feel like you're losing the battle for your kids' hearts. But here's the thing – kids are smarter than we often give them credit for. With time, patience, and a whole lot of love, they'll likely see through the smokescreen.

Your consistent love, respect, and presence in their lives will speak volumes louder than any poison your ex tries to pour in their ears.

Keep showing up, keep loving fiercely, and keep being the awesome mom or dad you are. Because at the end of the day, love trumps manipulation every single time.

LEGAL OPTIONS FOR CUSTODY AND VISITATION

Imagine standing before an enormous, bewildering maze. Its hedges tower overhead, paths twist and turn unpredictably, and somewhere at its heart lies your ultimate goal – a fair and nurturing arrangement for your children. But there's a catch: your ex-partner, the narcissist, is lurking within, setting traps and attempting to reshape the landscape at every turn. Welcome to the challenging world of co-parenting with a narcissist!

DIVORCING A NARCISSIST?

The temptation to turn tail and flee might be strong, but hold steady. Take a deep, centering breath. You're more prepared for this challenge than you realize, and you're not facing this complex journey alone. This chapter is your friendly companion, offering support and insights as you navigate this difficult terrain.

Let's talk custody lingo. It's like learning a new language, except instead of ordering coffee, you're fighting for your kids. Here's your crash course:

1. Legal Custody: This is the power to make big decisions about your kids' lives – think education, healthcare, and religion. It can be joint (you both decide) or sole (one parent calls the shots).

2. Physical Custody: This is about where your kids lay their heads at night. Again, it can be joint (kids split time between homes) or sole (kids primarily live with one parent).

3. Visitation: If one parent has sole physical custody, the other usually gets visitation rights. Think of it as your kids' travel schedule.

Now, in a perfect world, you and your ex would sit down, have a civilized chat, and work out a fair arrangement. But when you're dealing with a narcissist, "civilized" and "fair" aren't exactly in their vocabulary. So, what's a parent to do?

1. Mediation: Imagine sitting down with your ex and a neutral third party to hash out an agreement. Sometimes it works, even with narcissists. But keep your guard up – narcissists are masters of manipulation, and mediators aren't always trained to spot

it. Think of yourself as a detective in this scenario, always on the lookout for those sneaky narcissistic tricks. Remember, just because you're in mediation doesn't mean you have to agree to everything – it's okay to hit the pause button if something feels off or if you need to consult with your own attorney. Your peace of mind is worth more than a quick resolution, so trust your gut and don't be afraid to speak up if the mediation starts feeling like a one-sided game of chess.

2. Collaborative Law: It's like everyone agreeing to sit at the grown-up table and work things out. You, your ex, and your lawyers put on your cooperation hats and try to hammer out a settlement without dragging each other to court. Sounds nice, right? Here's the deal: you all agree to share info openly and hunt for solutions that won't leave anyone feeling like they got the short end of the stick. The catch? If this kumbaya session falls apart, you'll need to find new lawyers if you end up in court. It can be a great way to skip the courtroom drama and save some cash. But hold up – remember who you're dealing with. Your narcissistic ex might see this as another stage for their performance. Keep your eyes peeled for any funny business or sudden "forgetfulness" about agreements. Collaborative law can lead to smoother sailing, but with a narcissist on board, you might hit some choppy waters. Stay alert and trust your gut.

3. Litigation: When all else fails, it's time to let a judge decide. It's not ideal – it's expensive, time-consuming, and stressful. But sometimes, it's the only way to cut through a narcissist's games

and get a fair shake. Think of it as the divorce world's version of "Judge Judy," but with less TV drama and more real-life consequences. While it might feel like you're gearing up for battle, remember that the courtroom is actually a place where facts speak louder than charm or manipulation. So, gather your evidence, polish your truth, and get ready to stand your ground – this is your chance to have an impartial referee blow the whistle on any foul play. Just don't forget to breathe and maybe treat yourself to some ice cream after each hearing – you're doing great, champ!

Here are some strategies on how to tilt the scales in your favor:

1. Document Everything: And I mean everything. Every text, every email, every missed visitation. Your documentation is your secret weapon in court.

2. Get a Custody Evaluation: A mental health professional can assess both parents and the kids. If your ex truly is a narcissist, a good evaluator might pick up on it.

3. Consider Supervised Visitation: If your ex's behavior is harmful to the kids, you can ask for their visits to be supervised. It's like having a referee for parenting.

4. Ask for a Guardian ad Litem: Think of this as your child's very own superhero in the legal world. A Guardian ad Litem (GAL) is like a special investigator appointed by the court to be your child's voice and advocate. Here's what you need to know:

- Role: The GAL's job is to investigate and determine what's best for your child, independent of what either parent wants.

- Qualifications: Usually an attorney or mental health professional with special training in child welfare.

- Powers: They can interview your child, both parents, teachers, doctors, and anyone else relevant to your child's life.

- Report: The GAL presents their findings and recommendations to the court, which carries significant weight in the judge's decisions.

- Narcissist Kryptonite: A GAL can see through manipulation tactics and focus on facts, not charm or intimidation.

- Objectivity: They provide an unbiased perspective, which is crucial when dealing with a narcissist who may be skilled at manipulating others' perceptions.

- Cost: While there may be fees involved, many find the investment worthwhile for the protection it provides.

Having a GAL can be a game-changer when you're dealing with a narcissistic ex. They can uncover truths that might otherwise be buried under layers of manipulation, ensuring that decisions are made in your child's best interest, not based on who's the most convincing storyteller.

1. Push for Specific, Detailed Orders: The vaguer the court order, the more room for a narcissist to manipulate. Get everything spelled out in painful detail.

2. Consider Parallel Parenting: This is like co-parenting's cousin who doesn't like to socialize. Communication is limited and business-like, often via email or parenting apps. Interactions are structured and limited, like kid exchanges at neutral locations. It minimizes contact between you and your ex, reducing opportunities for conflict and manipulation. It's particularly useful when dealing with a high-conflict ex or a narcissist who thrives on drama. Parallel parenting lets you focus on your relationship with your kids, without getting entangled in unnecessary battles with your ex. It's not about being best buddies; it's about being the best parents you can be – separately.

Let's face it – there's no sugarcoating this bitter pill. Battling a narcissist in court is like undergoing a root canal while riding a rollercoaster during an earthquake. It's a special kind of torture that makes dental surgery look like a spa day. There will be days when you want to throw in the towel, days when you question if it's all worth it.

Remember this crucial truth – your battle extends far beyond yourself. You're standing up for your children, safeguarding their safety, protecting their well-being, and securing their future. And let's be crystal clear: that cause is always worth every ounce of your effort.

The legal system might move slowly, but it does move. With patience, persistence, and the right strategy, you can navigate this maze and come out the other side with a custody arrangement that protects you and your children.

So, straighten that invisible cape, channel your inner superhero, and get ready to conquer this legal labyrinth. Your kids are lucky to have a parent who fights so hard for them.

Let's shift gears and focus on nurturing your well-being during this legal marathon. You're the star athlete in this high-stakes game, and every champion needs proper training and recovery. Prioritizing your own care isn't a luxury – it's as essential as oxygen for your journey ahead!

CHAPTER 7

Rebuilding Your Self-Esteem

If you've made it this far, give yourself a pat on the back. No, seriously – do it right now. I'll wait.

Done? Good. Now, let's talk about you. Yes, YOU. Not your ex, not your kids, not the mountain of laundry that's been giving you the stink eye from the corner of your bedroom. Just you.

Remember that vibrant soul you used to be before the storm of narcissistic abuse rained all over your parade? The one who laughed without hesitation, who had dreams and opinions and favorite songs? That authentic self is still there, waiting in the wings. And it's high time to roll out the red carpet and welcome that true you back into the spotlight.

Welcome to Chapter 7, where we're going to rebuild your self-esteem from the ground up. Think of it as an extreme makeover, inner beauty edition. So grab a comfy seat, your favorite beverage, and let's get started on Project Awesome You and rebuild your self-esteem from shattered to spectacular!

RECOGNIZING YOUR WORTH BEYOND THE NARCISSIST'S PROJECTION

Let's dive right into the deep end and tackle the big, ugly monster lurking in the shadows of your mind. That voice in your head that sounds suspiciously like your ex, the one that whispers all sorts of nasty things about your worth? It's a liar, liar, pants on fire.

Narcissists are like funhouse mirrors. They reflect a distorted image that has nothing to do with reality and everything to do with their own insecurities. But you, my friend, are not that warped reflection.

You are the sum of your kindness, your resilience, your laugh lines, and yes, even your mistakes. You are the friend who shows up with ice cream after a breakup, the parent who checks for monsters under the bed, the coworker who remembers everyone's coffee order.

Exercise time! Grab a pen and paper (or your phone if you're feeling digitally inclined) and jot down five things you like about yourself. Stuck? Ask a friend or family member what they appreciate about you. Sometimes we need to borrow someone else's glasses to see ourselves clearly.

Your worth isn't determined by someone else's inability to see it. You are worthy of love, respect, and happiness simply because you exist. Full stop, no conditions apply.

TECHNIQUES FOR BOOSTING YOUR SELF-ESTEEM

Now that we've established you're pretty darn amazing (and don't you forget it), let's dive deeper into how to keep that self-esteem meter ticking upwards. Think of this as assembling your own personal cheerleading squad, pompoms optional but enthusiasm mandatory!

1. The Gratitude Game: Every night before bed, write down three things you're grateful for about yourself. Did you nail that presentation at work? Rock that parallel parking job? Successfully resist the siren call of the snooze button? Celebrate it!

    ○ Pro tip: Research shows that practicing gratitude can actually rewire your brain for more positivity. It's like giving your mind a happiness makeover!

2. Affirmation Station: Pick a positive affirmation that resonates with you. Something like "I am worthy of love and respect" or "I trust myself and my decisions." Repeat it to yourself in the mirror every morning. Feel silly? Good! Giggle away, but keep saying it.

    ○ Level up: Create a vision board with your affirmations and images that represent your best self. Visual cues can be powerful reminders of your worth.

3. The Accomplishment Jar: Get a jar (or a box, or a fancy hat – whatever floats your boat) and every time you accomplish something, write it down and pop it in. On tough days, pull out a few slips and remind yourself of your awesomeness.

- Bonus round: Include compliments you receive from others. Sometimes we need to borrow others' perspectives to see our true value.

4. Treat Yo' Self: Do something nice for yourself every day. It doesn't have to be big – a bubble bath, 10 minutes of uninterrupted reading time. You deserve good things, so start giving them to yourself.

    - Self-care challenge: Try a new form of self-care each week. Yoga, meditation, nature walks – explore what makes you feel nurtured and valued.

5. The Compliment Challenge: Give yourself one genuine compliment every day. Bonus points if you say it out loud!

    - Mirror work: Stand in front of a mirror, look yourself in the eye, and deliver that compliment. It might feel awkward at first, but it's a powerful way to rebuild your relationship with yourself.

6. Skill Building: Learn something new or improve an existing skill. Mastery experiences are fantastic for boosting self-esteem.

    - Start small: Learn to cook a new recipe, pick up a few phrases in a new language, or try a new workout routine. Each small win builds confidence.

7. The Comparison Detox: Unfollow social media accounts that make you feel less-than. Replace them with accounts that inspire

and uplift you.

- Reality check: Remember, social media is everyone's highlight reel. Your behind-the-scenes is not comparable to someone else's carefully curated public image.

8. Boundary Bootcamp: Practice setting and maintaining healthy boundaries. Each time you honor your own needs and limits, you're telling yourself that you matter.

- Start with small "no's": Decline a minor request that you'd usually agree to out of obligation. Notice how it feels to prioritize your own needs.

9. The Forgiveness Project: Work on forgiving yourself for past mistakes. We're all perfectly imperfect humans, after all.

- Try this: Write a letter of forgiveness to yourself. Be as kind and understanding as you would be to a dear friend.

10. Positivity Portfolio: Create a file (digital or physical) of positive memories, achievements, and kind words from others. Review it regularly, especially when you need a boost.

- Include tangible reminders: Concert tickets, certificates, photos of happy moments – anything that sparks joy and pride.

Building self-esteem is like working out – it might feel awkward and uncomfortable at first, but keep at it and you'll start seeing (and feeling) results. Your self-esteem is a muscle, and every time you practice these exercises, you're doing a rep. Before you know it, you'll be flexing that self-love like a pro!

On days when it feels tough, remember this: you've already survived 100% of your worst days. You're resilient, you're growing, and you're on your way to becoming the best version of yourself. So give yourself a high-five, do a little dance, and keep cheering yourself on. Your biggest fan? It's you, champ!

OVERCOMING NEGATIVE SELF-TALK

Ah, the inner critic. That delightful voice that pipes up just when you're feeling good about yourself to remind you of that embarrassing thing you did in third grade. Time to serve that naysayer an eviction notice!

First, let's get acquainted with your inner critic. What does it sound like? What does it usually say? Often, we'll find it sounds a lot like people from our past who were less than kind. Recognizing this can be a powerful first step in separating your true self from these internalized negative voices.

You don't have to believe everything you think. Mind-blowing, right? Just because that critical voice pipes up doesn't mean it's speaking truth. It's just a thought, and thoughts can be changed.

Let's expand our toolkit for showing that inner critic the door:

1. The Gratitude Flip: When your inner critic starts listing all your flaws, flip the script. For every negative point it raises, challenge yourself to find something you're grateful for about yourself. "I'm

so disorganized" becomes "I'm grateful for my creativity, which sometimes leads to a bit of chaos."

2. Positive Personality Playlist: Create a playlist of songs that make you feel confident and empowered. When negative self-talk strikes, blast your playlist and have a one-person dance party. It's hard to be down on yourself when you're grooving to "I'm Every Woman" or "Eye of the Tiger"!

3. The Compliment Collection: Start collecting compliments. When someone says something nice about you, write it down. When your inner critic gets loud, pull out your collection and read through it. It's like having a cheer squad in your pocket!

4. Mindfulness Meditation: Practice observing your thoughts without judgment. This can help you create some distance between yourself and your negative self-talk. Try this simple exercise: Close your eyes, focus on your breath, and imagine your thoughts as leaves floating down a stream. You don't need to grab them or push them away – just watch them pass.

5. The Scientific Method: Treat your negative self-talk like a hypothesis that needs testing. "I'm a failure" becomes "Let's examine the evidence for and against this claim." You might be surprised at how often your inner critic's "facts" don't stand up to scrutiny!

6. Language Matters: Pay attention to the language you use with yourself. Are you using absolute terms like "always" or "never"?

Challenge these. "I always mess up" becomes "Sometimes I make mistakes, and that's part of being human."

7. The Time Travel Test: When you're beating yourself up over something, ask yourself: "Will this matter in a year? In five years?" Often, we catastrophize small setbacks. This perspective can help you see the bigger picture.

8. Humor Therapy: Sometimes, the best way to deal with your inner critic is to laugh at it. Try saying its comments out loud in a silly voice. It's hard to take "You're such a loser" seriously when it's being said in a Mickey Mouse voice!

9. The Compassion Challenge: Practice extending the same compassion to yourself that you would to a small child or a beloved pet. If you wouldn't say it to them, don't say it to yourself.

10. The Success Journal: Keep a journal of your successes, big and small. Writing them down makes them more concrete and gives you a ready resource to combat negative self-talk.

Changing your self-talk is a process. It's like learning a new language – the language of self-love and compassion. You might not be fluent overnight, but with practice, you'll find yourself becoming more and more proficient.

And here's a fun fact to keep you motivated: Studies have shown that positive self-talk can actually improve your performance in various areas of life, from sports to public speaking to test-taking. So by working on your self-talk, you're not just making yourself feel better – you're literally setting yourself up for greater success!

So, the next time your inner critic pipes up, put on your imaginary referee whistle and call a foul on that negative play. You've got a whole playbook of strategies now, and with practice, you'll be running circles around that Negative Nancy in no time. Remember, you're the captain of this team, and you're playing to win – the game of self-love, that is!

SETTING HEALTHY BOUNDARIES IN FUTURE RELATIONSHIPS

Think of boundaries as your personal force field – they protect you from energy vampires and keep your newly rebuilt self-esteem safe and sound. They're like the bouncer at the VIP club of your life, deciding who and what gets in.

Setting boundaries might feel uncomfortable at first, especially if you're not used to it. But it's a game-changer. It's like upgrading your personal operating system to "Awesome 2.0". Let's expand our boundary-setting toolkit:

1. The Boundary Buffet: Different relationships require different boundaries. Think of it like a buffet – you wouldn't pile your plate the same way for breakfast as you would for dinner. With family, you might need emotional boundaries. With coworkers, perhaps professional boundaries. With friends, maybe time boundaries. Customize your boundary buffet for each relationship in your life.

2. The Broken Record Technique: When someone keeps pushing your boundaries, become a broken record. Calmly repeat your

boundary statement without getting drawn into arguments or explanations. "I understand you want to discuss this, but I'm not comfortable with that topic. Let's talk about something else."

3. The Boundary Barometer: Regularly check in with yourself. How do you feel after interactions with certain people? Energized or drained? Respected or dismissed? Your feelings are your internal boundary barometer – pay attention to them!

4. The Delayed Response: You don't always have to respond immediately when someone makes a request or demand. It's okay to say, "Let me think about that and get back to you." This gives you time to check in with yourself and your boundaries.

5. The Boundary Role Play: Practice setting boundaries in a safe environment. Role-play difficult conversations with a trusted friend or therapist. The more you practice, the more natural it will feel.

6. The Boundary Mantra: Create a personal mantra to remind yourself of the importance of your boundaries. Something like, "My boundaries are an act of self-love" or "Healthy boundaries make healthy relationships." Repeat as needed!

7. The Gradual Boundary: Sometimes, you might need to implement boundaries gradually, especially in long-standing relationships. Start with small boundaries and build up. It's like slowly turning up the thermostat instead of blasting the AC.

8. The Boundary Check-In: In new relationships, have regular boundary check-ins. "How are you feeling about our communication style?" "Is there anything you need more or less of from me?" This normalizes boundary discussions and keeps everyone on the same page.

9. The Non-Negotiables List: Create a list of your non-negotiable boundaries - the ones that are absolutely essential for your well-being. For instance, one crucial boundary might be: "My feelings are valid and deserve respect. I won't tolerate anyone dismissing, belittling, or mocking how I feel." Other non-negotiables could cover areas like personal space, time management, or financial decisions. Keep this list easily accessible – perhaps on your phone or pinned to your mirror. It's your quick reference guide for those moments when you need a reminder of your worth and your right to protect it.

10. The Boundary Celebration: Celebrate when you successfully set and maintain a boundary! Did you say no to an unreasonable request? Time for a personal happy dance! Reinforcing boundary-setting with positive associations helps make it a habit.

Boundaries are not about controlling others – they're about taking responsibility for your own well-being. They're not walls to keep people out, but guidelines to show people how to come in.

Setting boundaries isn't just good for you – it's good for your relationships too. Clear boundaries create clear expectations, which lead to healthier, more respectful interactions. It's like giving everyone a map of your personal terrain – no more accidentally stepping on landmines!

You might feel guilty when you start setting boundaries, especially with people who aren't used to them. That's normal! But your guilt doesn't mean you're doing something wrong. It often means you're doing something right that you're not used to doing. Think of it as growing pains for your self-esteem.

Lastly, be patient with yourself. Setting and maintaining boundaries is a skill, and like any skill, it takes practice. You wouldn't expect to nail a perfect soufflé on your first try, right? (And if you did, we need to talk about your secret culinary talents!) Same goes for boundaries. Keep at it, and soon you'll be a boundary-setting maestro.

So go ahead, flex those boundary-setting muscles. Adjust your force field. Polish that VIP velvet rope. You're the boss of your life, and you get to decide who and what has an all-access pass. Your future self – confident, respected, and thriving – is cheering you on. And trust me, that version of you? They're absolutely spectacular.

CHAPTER 8

REDISCOVERING YOURSELF

Remember that vibrant soul who used to dream big, laugh without restraint, and dance like no one was watching? That authentic self is still within you, waiting in the wings. It's time to roll out the red carpet and welcome that true you back into the spotlight.

After surviving a relationship with a narcissist and navigating the stormy waters of divorce, you might feel like a stranger to yourself. It's as if you've been living someone else's life, molded into a shape that doesn't quite fit. But this is your chance for a renaissance, a rebirth of the authentic you.

In this chapter, we're going to embark on an exciting journey of self-rediscovery. We'll dust off those long-forgotten passions, unearth buried dreams, and breathe new life into the person you were always meant to be. It's not about becoming someone new—it's about peeling away the layers of control and manipulation to reveal the vibrant, resilient you that's been there all along.

RECONNECTING WITH YOUR PASSIONS AND INTERESTS

Picture yourself standing in front of your closet, staring at that dusty guitar in the corner. Or maybe it's a pair of running shoes, a half-finished novel, or a neglected easel. Whatever it is, it's been sitting there, patiently waiting for you to remember the joy it once brought you. Well, guess what? Today's the day we blow off that dust and rekindle that spark!

Welcome to the "Reconnecting with Your Passions and Interests" portion of our journey. Think of it as your personal comeback tour, where you're both the headlining act and the screaming fan. Ready to rock? Let's dive in!

Let's talk about why reconnecting with your passions is so crucial. It's not just about having fun (although that's a pretty awesome bonus). Your interests and passions are like the secret sauce that makes you, well, you!

During your relationship with a narcissist, you might have felt like your identity was slowly being erased, replaced by a version of yourself that fit their narrative. Your passions and interests? They probably got shoved to the back burner, if not tossed out entirely.

Those passions, however, are a direct line to your authentic self. They're the things that light you up, that make time fly, that give you that "yes, this is what I'm meant to be doing" feeling. And rediscovering them? It's like finding pieces of a puzzle you didn't even realize was incomplete.

Alright, so you're on board with the idea, but maybe you're sitting there thinking, "That's great and all, but I can't even remember what I used to like doing." Don't worry, detective, we're about to embark on The Great Passion Scavenger Hunt!

1. The Time Machine Exercise: Close your eyes and think back to when you were a kid. What did you love doing? What could you spend hours on without getting bored? Sometimes our childhood passions hold clues to what truly lights us up.

2. The Envy Indicator: Pay attention to what makes you feel a twinge of envy when you see others doing it. That pang might be pointing you towards a forgotten passion.

3. The Bookshelf/Browser History Test: Take a look at your bookshelf or your browser history. What topics keep popping up? What do you find yourself constantly curious about?

4. The "If I Had All the Time and Money in the World" Game: Play a little game of make-believe. If you had unlimited resources, what would you spend your time doing?

5. The Joy Journal: For a week, jot down moments when you feel genuinely happy or engaged. Look for patterns – they might lead you to rediscovered passions.

This isn't about pressure or perfection. It's about exploration and rediscovery. Be open to surprises – you might find new passions you never knew you had!

So, you've identified some potential passions. Awesome! But maybe you're feeling a bit rusty, or unsure how to start. Don't worry, we've got you covered. Here's your roadmap to reigniting that spark:

1. Start Small: Don't pressure yourself to dive in headfirst. If you used to love painting, start with a small sketchpad and some pencils. Loved running? Begin with short walks. Baby steps are still steps forward!

2. Create a Passion Corner: Designate a specific area in your home for your rediscovered passion. Having a visible reminder can encourage you to engage with it more often.

3. Schedule Passion Time: Block out time in your calendar specifically for exploring your interests. Treat it like any other important appointment.

4. Find Your Tribe: Look for local groups or online communities centered around your interests. Connecting with others who share your passion can be incredibly motivating.

5. The Two-Minute Rule: If you're feeling resistant, commit to just two minutes of your chosen activity. Often, getting started is the hardest part.

6. Document Your Journey: Keep a journal or take photos of your progress. Seeing how far you've come can be a huge motivator.

7. Be Kind to Yourself: This is about joy and rediscovery, not perfection. Celebrate every small win along the way.

Sometimes, reconnecting with old passions can bring up difficult emotions. Maybe your ex criticized your hobby, or you associate certain activities with painful memories. It's okay to feel conflicted – it's all part of the healing process.

If you find yourself struggling, try these strategies:

1. Reframe the Narrative: Instead of "This reminds me of my ex," try "I'm reclaiming this for myself."

2. Create New Associations: Engage with your passion in a new location, with new people, or in a different way to create fresh, positive associations.

3. Seek Support: Consider talking to a therapist about any emotional blocks you're experiencing. They can provide strategies to work through these feelings.

4. Be Patient: Healing isn't linear. Some days will be easier than others, and that's perfectly normal.

As you start reconnecting with your passions and interests, you might notice something magical happening. It's what I like to call the Passion Snowball Effect. You start with one small interest, and before you know it, you're exploring new hobbies, meeting new people, and feeling more like yourself than you have in years.

This snowball effect isn't just about hobbies – it's about rediscovering your zest for life. It's about remembering that you are a complex, interesting, passionate person with so much to offer the world.

So go ahead, pick up that guitar, lace up those running shoes, dust off that easel. Your passions have been waiting for you, and trust me, they're just as excited for this reunion as you are.

This journey of rediscovery is uniquely yours. Embrace the process, celebrate the small victories, and most importantly, have fun with it! You're not just reconnecting with your passions – you're reconnecting with yourself. And that, my friend, is the greatest comeback tour of all.

BUILDING A SUPPORT NETWORK

Imagine yourself standing at the edge of a cliff, ready to take a leap into the unknown world of post-narcissist life. Scary, right? Now imagine the same scene, but this time, you're strapped into a harness, surrounded by a team of expert climbers, all cheering you on. Feels a whole lot better, doesn't it?

Welcome to the "Building a Support Network" section, where we're going to assemble your personal dream team. Think of it as creating your very own Avengers squad, but instead of fighting alien invasions, they're helping you navigate the thrilling (and sometimes terrifying) journey of rediscovering yourself. Ready to start recruiting? Let's dive in!

Let's talk about why having a solid support network is crucial. And no, it's not just about having people to share memes with (although that's a delightful bonus).

A strong support network is like a Swiss Army knife for your emotional wellbeing. It's a shoulder to cry on, a cheerleader for your victories, a sounding board for your ideas, and sometimes, a much-needed reality check. In the aftermath of a relationship with a narcissist, these connections can be literal lifelines.

Research shows that people with strong social support systems are more resilient, have better mental health outcomes, and even have stronger immune systems. So, we're not just talking about warm fuzzies here – we're talking about your overall health and happiness.

Now, it's understandable if some of you are thinking: "That's great, but I don't have a support network. My ex isolated me from everyone I knew." If that's you, take a moment to recognize your incredible bravery in taking this step towards healing. You deserve a standing ovation for your courage. And here's some good news – it's entirely possible to build a network from the ground up, even if you're starting from scratch.

1. Reconnect with Old Friends: Remember those friends your ex didn't like? It might be time to shoot them a message. You'd be surprised how many people will be thrilled to hear from you.

2. Family Ties: If you have supportive family members, now's the time to lean on them. They've probably been waiting for the chance to help.

3. Support Groups: Look for local or online support groups for survivors of narcissistic abuse. These folks get it in a way others might not.

4. Hobby-Based Connections: Remember those passions we talked about earlier? Pursue them in group settings. Shared interests are a great foundation for new friendships.

5. Professional Support: Therapists, counselors, and life coaches can be invaluable members of your support network.

6. Online Communities: Join forums or social media groups related to your interests or experiences. Just remember to practice safe internet habits!

7. Volunteer: Helping others can be a great way to help yourself. Plus, you'll meet like-minded individuals.

Building a network takes time. Be patient with yourself and celebrate each new connection you make.

When it comes to your support network, bigger isn't always better. What you're aiming for is a carefully curated group of individuals who truly have your back. Think of it as the difference between a Walmart and a boutique shop – sure, Walmart has everything, but that boutique is going to give you personalized, quality service.

So, how do you ensure you're building a quality network? Here are some tips:

1. The Energy Check: After interacting with someone, check in with yourself. Do you feel energized or drained? Stick with the energizers.

2. The Reciprocity Rule: Healthy relationships involve give and take. Are your interactions balanced, or are you always the one giving (or taking)?

3. The Growth Factor: Look for people who encourage your growth and celebrate your successes without jealousy.

4. The Safety Test: You should feel safe being vulnerable with the core members of your support network. If you're always on guard, something's off.

5. The Respect Requirement: This one's non-negotiable. Every member of your network should treat you with respect.

6. The Diversity Bonus: Try to build a network with diverse perspectives and skills. You never know what kind of support you might need.

Congratulations! You've started building your support network. But a support network is a living thing. It needs care and attention to thrive. Here's how to keep your network healthy and strong:

1. Stay in Touch: Regular contact is key. Set reminders if you need to.

2. Be There for Them: Support is a two-way street. Be ready to offer help when your network needs it.

3. Express Gratitude: Let your support network know how much you appreciate them. A little thanks goes a long way.

4. Respect Boundaries: Just as you're setting healthy boundaries, respect the boundaries of others.

5. Keep It Real: Authenticity is the fertilizer that helps relationships

grow. Don't be afraid to show your true self.

6. Plan Group Activities: Organize get-togethers or group outings to strengthen bonds within your network.

Building and maintaining a support network isn't always smooth sailing. You might encounter a few storms along the way:

1. The Over-Helper: Someone who's always trying to "fix" you. Gently remind them that sometimes you just need a listening ear.

2. The Negative Nancy: If someone consistently brings you down, it might be time to reevaluate their role in your network.

3. The Boundary Pusher: Some people might not respect your new boundaries. Stand firm – those who truly support you will understand.

4. The Ghost: People who disappear when things get tough. It's okay to let these connections fade.

5. The Narcissist Sympathizer: Unfortunately, some people might not understand your experience. It's okay to limit your interactions with them.

It's okay to outgrow relationships or realize that some connections aren't serving you anymore. Your support network should evolve as you do.

As you continue on your journey of rediscovery, your support network will be there, cheering you on, picking you up when you stumble, and celebrating every victory, big and small.

Building a strong support network is one of the most powerful things you can do for yourself in the aftermath of narcissistic abuse. It's a declaration to the world – and more importantly, to yourself – that you are worthy of love, support, and genuine connections.

So go forth and build your dream team. Your future self is already thanking you. And if all else fails, you've always got me, your friendly neighborhood author, cheering you on from the pages of this book.

DATING AFTER NARCISSISTIC ABUSE

The very thought of dating again might send shivers down your spine or make your stomach do somersaults. That's completely normal. After all, your last relationship was a masterclass in manipulation and emotional turmoil. But not everyone out there is a narcissist, and you are now armed with wisdom and strength you didn't have before.

Let's start by addressing the obvious: fear. It's okay to be scared. In fact, a healthy dose of caution can be your ally. But we don't want fear to be the architect of your future. Instead, we'll use it as a tool to build a stronger, more discerning you.

Before you even think about trusting someone else, it's crucial to rebuild trust in yourself. You might be questioning your judgment right now, thinking, "How did I not see the red flags?" or "What if I fall for the same type again?" These doubts are part of the healing process, but they don't define you.

Here's a little exercise to help you reconnect with your intuition:

1. Find a quiet moment and think back to your relationship with the narcissist.

2. Try to recall moments when you felt something was off, even if you pushed those feelings aside.

3. Write down these instances, acknowledging that your intuition was trying to protect you.

4. Reflect on how you've grown and what you've learned since then.

This exercise isn't about dwelling on the past; it's about recognizing that your inner voice was there all along. Now, you're in a position to listen to it more closely and trust it more fully.

If there's one invaluable lesson to take from your experience, it's the importance of boundaries. In your journey of rediscovery, think of boundaries as your personal forcefield—they protect your energy, values, and sense of self.

Before you step into the dating world, take some time to define your non-negotiables. These aren't just about deal-breakers in a potential partner; they're about how you want to be treated and what you're willing to accept in any relationship, romantic or otherwise.

Here are some questions to ponder:

- What behaviors will you no longer tolerate?

- How do you want to feel in a healthy relationship?

- What are your core values that you're not willing to compromise?

Write these down and keep them close. They're not just guidelines for future relationships; they're affirmations of your worth and reminders of the strong person you've become.

After the whirlwind of a narcissistic relationship, you might find yourself craving connection. That's natural—we're wired for companionship. But here's where we flip the script: instead of rushing into something new, we're going to savor the journey of getting to know someone (and yourself) slowly.

Think of it like this: you're not just dating to find a partner; you're dating to learn about yourself, to practice setting boundaries, and to enjoy the process of connection without pressure. Here are some tips to keep in mind:

1. Be upfront about your pace: It's okay to tell someone you want to take things slow. The right person will respect your boundaries.

2. Focus on friendship first: Build a foundation of trust and mutual respect before considering a romantic relationship.

3. Keep your independence: Continue nurturing your friendships, hobbies, and personal growth. A healthy relationship adds to your life; it doesn't become your whole life.

4. Trust your gut: If something feels off, it probably is. Don't ignore those instincts—they're your emotional immune system at work.

5. Seek support: Keep your support network close. Share your experiences with trusted friends or your therapist. They can offer valuable outside perspectives.

There's no rush. You're not just looking for any relationship; you're opening yourself up to the possibility of a healthy, nurturing connection. And that starts with nurturing your relationship with yourself.

In the next sections, we'll explore how to recognize healthy relationship dynamics, how to spot red flags early on, and most importantly, how to keep flourishing as an individual while opening your heart to new possibilities. Your journey of rediscovery is just beginning, and the best chapters of your life are yet to be written.

CREATING A VISION FOR YOUR NEW LIFE

Alright, my friend, take a deep breath. Feel that? That's the sweet air of possibility filling your lungs. We've talked about rediscovering yourself and dipping your toes back into the dating pool, but now it's time for the really exciting part: envisioning your future.

When you were a kid, and adults would ask, "What do you want to be when you grow up?" Well, guess what? You get to ask yourself that question again, but this time with the wisdom and experience you've gained. How cool is that?

Find a quiet spot, grab your favorite writing supplies (or use your device) and start brainstorming, and let your imagination run wild. Don't censor yourself, don't worry about practicality just yet. We're dreaming here, and in dreams, anything is possible.

Ask yourself:

- If you could design your perfect day, what would it look like?
- What kind of work would make you excited to get out of bed in the morning?
- Where do you see yourself living? In a bustling city, a quiet suburb, or maybe on a beach?
- What hobbies or passions have you always wanted to explore?
- How do you want to feel every day when you wake up?

Write it all down, no matter how outlandish it might seem. Want to learn to tango in Argentina? Put it on the list. Dreaming of starting your own business? Jot it down. Yearning to adopt a pet sloth? (Okay, maybe check local laws on that one, but you get the idea!)

Now that you've let your imagination soar, let's bring those dreams down to earth and start turning them into achievable goals. Don't worry, we're not going to squash your dreams – we're going to give them roots so they can grow.

1. Prioritize Your Dreams: Look at your list and identify the top 3-5 things that resonate with you the most. These are your big-picture goals.

2. Break It Down: For each of these goals, brainstorm smaller, actionable steps you can take to move towards them. Want to change careers? Maybe the first step is updating your resume or taking an online course in your field of interest.

3. Set Timelines: Give yourself realistic deadlines for these smaller steps. We're building a new life here, not racing against the clock. Be kind to yourself in your planning.

4. Create a Vision Board: Whether it's a physical board or a digital collage on Pinterest, visualizing your goals can be incredibly powerful. Cut out or pin pictures, quotes, or anything that represents your dreams and arrange them in a way that inspires you.

Here's a little secret: the joy isn't just in reaching your destination; it's in the journey itself. As you work towards your vision, you'll discover new things about yourself, meet interesting people, and have experiences you never imagined.

This vision isn't set in stone. As you grow and change, your dreams might shift too, and that's perfectly okay. The important thing is that you're moving forward, guided by your own desires and aspirations, not someone else's expectations or limitations.

It's natural to wonder, "But what if I fail?" or "Do I really deserve this?" Those doubts are normal but they don't get to drive the car. You do.

When doubts creep in:

1. Acknowledge them. Say, "I hear you, but you're not in charge anymore."

2. Remind yourself of how far you've come. You've survived a narcissistic relationship and divorce – you're basically a superhero.

3. Reach out to your support network. Sometimes we need a cheerleader, and that's okay.

4. Review your vision board or your written goals. Reconnect with why you're doing this.

As you embark on this journey of creating your new life, don't forget to celebrate your progress – no matter how small it might seem. Finished updating your resume? That calls for your favorite dessert. Signed up for a dance class? Time for a little happy dance of your own.

Each step forward is a victory, a testament to your resilience and determination. You're not just surviving anymore; you're thriving, creating, and growing. And it looks fantastic on you.

So, my brave friend, what's your vision? What incredible adventures await you in this next chapter of your life? The pen is in your hand, and the story is yours to write. Make it a bestseller.

CHAPTER 9

Healing and Moving Forward

Imagine yourself standing at the base of a mountain. The peak seems impossibly far away, shrouded in mist. The path ahead is winding, sometimes steep, and occasionally obscured. But you've already climbed further than you realize. That mountain? It's your healing journey, and you're already on your way up.

Welcome to Chapter 9, brave adventurer. We're about to embark on the most transformative part of your journey – understanding and embracing the healing process. Don't worry if you're feeling a mix of excitement and trepidation; that's perfectly normal. Recovery is a unique process for each person, often involving progress and setbacks. There's no set timeline or predetermined path - your journey is your own. It's a deeply personal odyssey, unique to each survivor. But the view from the top is worth every step.

UNDERSTANDING THE HEALING PROCESS

Healing from narcissistic abuse isn't like recovering from a cold. There's no "take two of these and call me in the morning" quick fix. It's more like tending to a garden – it requires patience, consistent care, and sometimes, getting your hands a little dirty. But oh, the beauty that blooms when you put in the work!

Let's debunk a major myth: healing doesn't happen in neat, orderly stages. You might have heard about the five stages of grief – denial, anger, bargaining, depression, and acceptance. While these can be part of the process, healing from narcissistic abuse is often more like a spiraling dance than a straight line.

Some days, you'll feel on top of the world, ready to conquer anything. Other days, a song on the radio or a familiar scent might send you tumbling back into a whirlpool of memories. This. Is. Normal. I repeat: This is normal, and it doesn't mean you're failing or backsliding. It means you're human, and you're processing complex emotions and experiences.

Think of healing like cleaning out an overstuffed closet. You might start with enthusiasm, making great progress, only to uncover a box of old photos that stops you in your tracks. You might spend time reminiscing, crying, or even considering shoving everything back in and slamming the door shut. But each item you sort through, each memory you process, brings you closer to a cleaner, more organized space – both in your closet and in your heart.

If your best friend was going through this healing process, how would you treat her? Would you berate her for having a bad day? Scold her for not "getting over it" fast enough? Of course not! You'd offer her compassion, understanding, and probably a giant tub of her favorite ice cream.

So why, oh why, are we often so much harder on ourselves? It's time to become your own best friend, your own cheerleader, your own comfort blanket. Self-compassion isn't self-indulgence; it's a crucial part of the healing process.

Try placing your hand over your heart and say to yourself, "I am healing at my own pace, and that's okay. I am doing the best I can with what I have right now." Feel a bit silly? Do it anyway. The more you practice self-compassion, the more natural it becomes.

In our goal-oriented world, it's easy to focus on big, dramatic changes and overlook the small victories. But healing is often made up of these tiny triumphs. Did you set a boundary today? Victory! Did you choose self-care over people-pleasing? Touchdown! Did you recognize a trigger and respond in a healthy way? Pop the champagne!

Use the journal provided in this book or create your own. Each day, write down one thing you're proud of, no matter how small it might seem. On tough days, flip through this journal. It's tangible proof of your progress, a reminder of how far you've come when the path ahead seems daunting.

While self-help books (like this one!) and support groups can be invaluable, there's no substitute for professional help when dealing with the aftermath of narcissistic abuse. A trained therapist, particularly one experienced in trauma and narcissistic abuse, can provide tools and insights tailored to your specific situation.

Think of it this way: If you broke your leg, you wouldn't just read a book on bone-setting and call it a day. You'd seek a professional to ensure proper healing. Your emotional and psychological well-being deserves the same level of expert care.

Seeking help isn't a sign of weakness; it's a sign of immense strength and self-awareness. It's you actively participating in your healing journey, and that's something to be incredibly proud of.

As we dive deeper into the healing process in the coming sections, know that healing isn't about erasing the past or pretending it didn't happen. It's about integrating your experiences into the tapestry of your life, learning from them, and using that knowledge to create a future that truly resonates with your authentic self.

You're not just healing; you're evolving, growing, and becoming a version of yourself that's stronger, wiser, and more vibrant than ever before. The journey might be challenging, but you've already proven you have the strength to face it head-on.

So, courageous one, are you ready to continue this healing adventure? Lace up your metaphorical hiking boots, pack your self-compassion, and let's explore the winding, beautiful path of healing together. The view from the top? It's breathtaking, and it's waiting for you.

FORGIVENESS VS. LETTING GO

Let's tackle the big F-word that often comes up in discussions about healing: Forgiveness. Just reading that word might make your stomach churn or your fists clench. I get it. The idea of forgiving someone who has caused you so much pain can feel like you're letting them off the hook or invalidating your own experiences. But forgiveness and letting go aren't the same thing, and neither one is mandatory for your healing journey.

Forgiveness is a personal choice, not a obligation. There's a pervasive myth that you must forgive to heal, but that's like saying you need to run a marathon to be healthy. Sure, it works for some people, but it's not the only path to wellness.

Forgiveness, in its truest form, is about releasing the anger and resentment you hold towards someone who has wronged you. It's not about condoning their actions or pretending they didn't hurt you. It's about freeing yourself from the emotional burden of carrying that anger.

But forgiveness is a process, and it's okay if you're not there yet - or if you never get there at all. Your healing isn't contingent on your ability to forgive your abuser.

Imagine you're holding onto a hot coal, intending to throw it at someone who hurt you. Who's getting burned while you hold onto it? That's right - you are. Letting go is about dropping that coal, not because the other person deserves relief, but because your hands deserve to heal.

Letting go means:

1. Accepting that you can't change the past

2. Recognizing that holding onto anger primarily hurts you, not your abuser

3. Choosing to focus your energy on your present and future, rather than dwelling on past hurts

It's not about forgetting or excusing what happened. It's about deciding that your abuser no longer gets to rent space in your head for free.

You don't have to choose between totally forgiving and remaining bitter. There's a whole spectrum of healing in between. You might reach a point where you can acknowledge what happened without it consuming your thoughts. Or you might find peace in accepting that what happened was unequivocally wrong, and that it's okay to feel angry about it sometimes.

Try this exercise: Write a letter to your abuser (that you'll never send). Pour out all your hurt, anger, and resentment onto the page. Then, write a letter to yourself, acknowledging your pain and affirming your right to heal on your own terms. Which letter feels more cathartic? Which one moves you forward?

Sometimes, understanding the psychology behind narcissistic behavior can help in the letting go process. It doesn't excuse their actions, but it can help you see that their behavior was about their own brokenness, not your worth.

Narcissists often act from a place of deep insecurity and a fragile sense of self. Their abusive behavior is a maladaptive way of trying to feel powerful and in control. Understanding this can help you see that their actions reflect their limitations, not your value.

Whether you choose to work towards forgiveness, focus on letting go, or find your own middle ground, the most important thing is this: you're in charge now. You get to decide what healing looks like for you. You're no longer a victim of your circumstances; you're the author of your own story.

Healing isn't about reaching a perfect state of zen-like calm where nothing ever bothers you. It's about building resilience, understanding yourself better, and creating a life that's aligned with your values and desires.

TURNING PAIN INTO PERSONAL GROWTH

Pause for a moment and take a good look in the mirror. See that person staring back at you? That's a certified superhero in disguise. You've weathered storms, climbed mountains, and emerged from the shadows of a relationship that tried to eclipse your brilliance. Now, it's time for your grand unveiling. We're about to embark on an incredible journey of transformation, turning the challenges you've faced into stepping stones for personal growth. It's like you've been a caterpillar, wrapped in a cocoon of adversity, and now you're ready to spread your wings. Get ready to soar, butterfly - your metamorphosis begins now.

You've probably heard the story of the phoenix – that mythical bird that bursts into flames only to rise again from its own ashes, more beautiful and powerful than before. Guess what? That's you. Your narcissistic relationship and divorce were the fire, and now it's time for your rise.

But here's the thing about rising from the ashes – it's not automatic. It takes intention, effort, and a whole lot of courage. The good news? You've already proven you have all of that in spades.

The first step in turning pain into growth is changing the narrative. You're not "damaged goods" or a "failed marriage statistic." You're a survivor, a warrior, a woman who looked adversity in the eye and said, "Not today, Satan."

Try writing down your story but with a twist. Instead of focusing on what was done to you, focus on how you responded, what you learned, and how you grew. For example:

- Instead of "I was manipulated and controlled," try "I learned to trust my own judgment and set firm boundaries."
- Rather than "My confidence was shattered," say "I'm rebuilding my self-esteem on a foundation of self-love and authenticity."

See the difference? It's not about denying the pain you experienced; it's about focusing on your strength and growth in response to that pain.

Have you heard of the growth mindset? It's the belief that your abilities and intelligence can be developed through effort, learning, and persistence. It's the opposite of a fixed mindset, which believes that our qualities are set in stone.

Adopting a growth mindset is like giving yourself permission to be a work in progress – and we're all works in progress. It means seeing challenges as opportunities to learn and grow, rather than insurmountable obstacles.

Here's how to cultivate a growth mindset:

1. Embrace challenges: See them as opportunities to grow stronger.

2. Learn from criticism: Use it as feedback to improve, not as a personal attack.

3. Find lessons in setbacks: Ask yourself, "What can I learn from this?"

4. Celebrate others' successes: Let them inspire you rather than threaten you.

5. Use the power of "yet": Instead of "I can't do this," try "I can't do this yet."

Newsflash: You have superpowers. Yes, you! Your experiences have given you unique strengths and insights. Maybe you've developed an uncanny ability to read people, or perhaps you've become an expert at managing stress. These are your superpowers, and it's time to recognize and cultivate them.

Make a list of the strengths you've developed through your experiences. These might include:

- Resilience

- Emotional intelligence

- Self-reliance

- Boundary-setting skills

- Intuition

- Adaptability

Now, think about how you can use these superpowers in other areas of your life. How can your newfound boundary-setting skills improve your work life? How can your resilience help you tackle new challenges?

You've probably heard of post-traumatic stress, but have you heard of post-traumatic growth? It's a psychological phenomenon where people who have experienced traumatic events undergo positive life changes as a result. It doesn't negate the pain you've experienced, but it does mean that growth and pain can coexist.

Areas of post-traumatic growth often include:

1. Greater appreciation of life

2. Closer relationships with supportive others

3. Increased sense of personal strength

4. Recognition of new possibilities in life

5. Spiritual or existential growth

Reflect on these areas in your own life. Have you experienced growth in any of them? Remember, growth doesn't mean you never feel pain or sadness about what happened. It means you're creating meaning and positive change alongside those feelings.

One powerful way to transform pain into growth is by using your experiences to help others and pay it forward. This could take many forms:

- Volunteering at a women's shelter

- Starting a support group for survivors of narcissistic abuse

- Writing a blog about your healing journey

- Becoming an advocate for domestic abuse awareness

By helping others, you reclaim your power and give new meaning to your experiences. Plus, there's scientific evidence that helping others can boost your own wellbeing and life satisfaction. Win-win!

As we wrap up this section, let's pack your growth toolkit:

1. Journaling: Write about your experiences, feelings, and growth.

2. Mindfulness practices: Stay present and cultivate self-awareness.

3. Continued learning: Read books, attend workshops, never stop growing.

4. Creative expression: Use art, music, or dance to process your emotions.

5. Physical self-care: Nourish your body with good food, exercise, and rest.

6. Connections: Surround yourself with supportive, positive people.

Turning pain into growth isn't about pretending the pain never happened. It's about choosing to use that pain as a catalyst for positive change in your life.

So, are you ready to alchemize your pain into personal gold? The journey might not always be easy but it's worth it. You're not just healing; you're evolving into the strongest, wisest, most authentic version of yourself. And know that you are absolutely magnificent.

SUCCESS STORIES: BEACONS OF HOPE ON YOUR HEALING JOURNEY

Alright, my brave friend, grab a cup of your favorite tea, find a cozy spot, and let's dive into some stories that'll light a fire in your heart. You know those moments when you're watching a movie, and the underdog finally wins? That surge of "Yeah! If they can do it, so can I!"? Well, that's what we're aiming for here. These are stories of survivors just like you who've walked through the fire and come out not just stronger, but thriving. They're proof that there's not just light at the end of the tunnel, but a whole dazzling world waiting for you.

Sarah's Symphony: From Silence to Center Stage

Picture Sarah, a 38-year-old music teacher who'd always dreamed of performing. But for years, her narcissistic ex-husband's voice echoed in her head: "You're a pathetic excuse for a musician. No one would ever want to hear you play. You're a waste of space, Sarah." She'd shrunk herself, silenced her voice, both literally and figuratively.

The divorce was a devastating storm, leaving Sarah feeling like a discarded instrument. But one day, while rummaging through her closet (isn't it funny how often breakthroughs happen during the most mundane tasks?), she found her old violin. With trembling hands and a heart heavy with doubt, she lifted it to her chin and played a single, wavering note.

That note became her lifeline. Sarah started small, playing for herself, then for her students. She joined a local orchestra, her confidence blossoming with each rehearsal. Two years after her divorce, Sarah stood on a stage, performing a solo piece she'd written herself. As the last note faded and the audience erupted in applause, Sarah realized she'd found her voice again – and it was more powerful, more vibrant, than ever before.

Today, Sarah runs a music therapy program for survivors of domestic abuse, helping others rediscover their voices through music. "Every time I pick up my violin," Sarah says, tears welling up in her eyes, "I'm reminded that I'm the composer of my own life's symphony. And I'm not going to let anyone silence me again."

Molly's Mural: Painting a New Reality

Molly's story starts in a colorless world. Her ex-husband, a successful businessman and covert narcissist, had slowly chipped away at her vibrant personality, leaving her feeling trapped in a world of self-doubt and anxiety. At 45, newly divorced and feeling lost, Molly couldn't even remember the last time she'd picked up a paintbrush.

It was her 10-year-old daughter who sparked the change. "Mom," she said one day, her eyes sparkling with excitement, "our walls are boring. Can we paint them?" Those innocent words were like a splash of color in Molly's gray world, a reminder of the vibrant life she once knew.

They started small, with Molly's daughter's room. But as Molly mixed colors and created designs, something awakened in her – a spark of creativity ignited, and the first rays of hope began to shine through the darkness. She enrolled in a local art class, ignoring the voice in her head that sounded suspiciously like her ex, telling her she was wasting her time.

Fast forward three years, and Molly's life is a canvas of vivid hues. She's become a sought-after mural artist, transforming bland city walls into stories of hope and resilience. Her proudest achievement? A community project where she guided other abuse survivors in creating a massive mural titled "Blooming Through Concrete." As they painted, Molly watched their faces transform, their eyes lighting up with a newfound confidence. It was a powerful reminder of the healing power of art, and a testament to the strength she had found within herself.

"Every brushstroke breathes life back into the parts of me I thought were lost forever," Molly shares, her eyes glistening with a mixture of tears and determination. Her voice, once timid, now resonates with newfound strength. "I'm not just painting walls. I'm rediscovering the vibrant hues of my soul, finally free to express myself without fear. It's like... it's like I'm coming home to myself after being lost for so long. And oh, the beauty I'm finding there - it's breathtaking."

Zoe's Zenith: Climbing to New Heights

Zoe's story is one of literal and metaphorical heights. Once an avid rock climber, Zoe had given up her passion during her 12-year marriage to a narcissistic man who systematically chipped away at her confidence, belittling her interests and demanding her undivided attention. At 50, freshly divorced, Zoe stood at the base of what seemed an insurmountable cliff, her spirit as eroded as the rocks she once loved to climb. Her eyes, once bright with adventure, had dulled from years of emotional abuse.

Her turning point came during a tear-filled therapy session. Her therapist, noticing Zoe's slumped shoulders and downcast eyes, gently asked, "If you could do anything right now, without fear of judgment, what would it be?" Zoe's immediate answer caught in her throat, surprising even her, "I'd climb a mountain." The words felt foreign on her tongue, yet familiar to her heart - a bittersweet reminder of the vibrant woman she once was.

Two months later, trembling with a mixture of fear and exhilaration, Zoe stood at the base of a beginner's climbing route. Her heart raced, not just from physical exertion, but from the emotional weight of this moment. It took her an hour to ascend what she once would have scaled in minutes. But when she reached the top, the vista before her blurred as tears of triumph welled in her eyes. For the first time in years, Zoe felt truly alive.

Zoe's journey back to herself wasn't just about climbing rocks. It was about scaling the mountains of self-doubt. She started a "Silver Scalers" group, encouraging other women over 50 to rediscover their strength through climbing.

Five years post-divorce, Zoe led an all-women expedition to Kilimanjaro. Standing at the summit, she realized she had climbed far higher than any mountain – she had ascended to the peak of her own power, reclaiming the identity that had been slowly stolen from her over the years.

"Every climb reminds me that I'm stronger than any obstacle," Zoe says, her voice filled with a sense of wonder and accomplishment. "And the view from the top? It's breathtaking. It's a testament to every woman's ability to rise above her past."

The Common Thread: Your Story in the Making

Sarah, Mollly, and Zoe's stories are unique, but they share common threads – threads that probably resonate with your own journey:

1. They all started small, with one note, one brushstroke, one step.

2. They rekindled the flames of passion their narcissistic partners had tried to extinguish.

3. They turned their healing into a way to help others.

4. They redefined success on their own terms.

But it's important to remember that these women aren't superhuman. They had doubts, setbacks, and days when getting out of bed felt like climbing Everest. The difference? They kept going, one day at a time. They refused to let their past define their future. They refused to let fear hold them back. They refused to give up on themselves.

Your success story is already in progress. Yes, you. The very fact that you're reading this, seeking to understand and heal, is a triumph. You're writing your story with every choice you make, every boundary you set, every moment you choose yourself. And the best part? You're the author, the hero, and the protagonist of your own narrative.

So, what will your story be? Will you compose a symphony of self-love like Sarah? Paint your world in vibrant hues like Molly? Or climb to new heights like Zoe? Whatever you choose, know that your story matters. And your best chapters? They're still to come.

Know that healing isn't a destination; it's a journey. And on this journey, you're not just surviving – you're authoring a masterpiece of resilience, growth, and triumph. So pick up that pen (or paintbrush, or violin, or climbing rope) and keep writing. Your success story is unfolding, and it's extraordinary.

CHAPTER 10

Embracing Single Parenthood

If you've made it to this chapter, you're not just a survivor of narcissistic abuse and divorce - you're also tackling one of life's most rewarding yet challenging roles: single parenthood. Before we dive in, take a moment to acknowledge your strength. You're doing an amazing job navigating this complex journey.

Single parenthood is a whirlwind of responsibilities, emotions, and never-ending tasks. It's like you've suddenly been handed a job that requires the skills of ten different professionals, all while operating on minimal sleep and maximum love. The demands are relentless, the hours are long, and the pay... well, let's just say the rewards aren't always immediately visible. But here's the incredible part: you're rising to this monumental challenge every single day. Your strength, resilience, and unwavering commitment to your children are nothing short of awe-inspiring.

In this chapter, we're going to explore the unique challenges you face as a single parent recovering from narcissistic abuse, and more importantly, we'll discover strategies to help you thrive in this new chapter of your life. Remember, you're not just surviving – you're laying the foundation for a beautiful, healthy future for you and your children.

NAVIGATING THE SINGLE PARENT LANDSCAPE

Welcome to the wild and wonderful world of single parenthood! It's a landscape filled with both challenges and incredible opportunities for growth. Let's start by acknowledging some of the common hurdles you might be facing:

- Time management (because who couldn't use a few extra hours in the day, right?)

- Financial pressures (those little ones sure know how to keep our wallets busy!)

- Emotional exhaustion (because being both mom and dad is no small feat)

- Guilt (oh hello, old friend - we see you lurking there)

- Loneliness (even when you're surrounded by little people 24/7)

Sound familiar? Don't worry, you're not alone, and we're going to tackle each of these head-on.

First things first: it's okay to admit that this is tough. In fact, acknowledging the challenges is the first step to finding solutions. You're human, after all, not superhuman (though you're pretty close!).

Here's a little exercise to help you gain perspective:

1. Grab a piece of paper and draw a line down the middle.

2. On one side, list your current challenges as a single parent.

3. On the other side, write down one strength you have that can help with each challenge.

This exercise isn't about solving everything immediately. It's about recognizing that for every challenge you face, you have inner resources to help you cope. You've survived narcissistic abuse – that alone is proof of your incredible resilience and strength.

Remember, the single parent landscape may be tough to navigate, but it's also rich with opportunities for personal growth, deeper connections with your children, and the chance to build the life you truly want – free from narcissistic abuse.

THE ART OF PRIORITY JUGGLING

Alright, let's talk priorities. When everything feels urgent, how do you decide what truly needs your attention? It's time to master the art of priority juggling!

First, let's introduce a tool I like to call the "Single Parent Priority Pyramid":

1. At the base: Basic needs (food, shelter, safety)

2. Next level: Your kids' well-being (emotional and physical)

3. Middle: Your own well-being (yes, you read that right!)

4. Upper middle: Work and financial stability

5. Top: Everything else

Notice where your well-being sits? It's not at the bottom, and it's not an afterthought. That's because taking care of yourself isn't selfish - it's necessary. You can't give your best if you're not at your best.

Now, let's look at some practical strategies for managing your many priorities:

1. Use a planner or a scheduling app: This can help you keep track of everyone's activities, appointments, and deadlines. Color-code for each family member to get a visual overview of your week.

2. Embrace the power of 'no': It's okay to decline non-essential commitments. Your energy is precious – use it wisely.

3. Involve your kids: Assign age-appropriate chores. It teaches responsibility and lightens your load. Win-win!

4. Batch similar tasks: Try meal prepping for the week on Sundays, or tackle all your phone calls in one sitting.

5. Set realistic expectations: Perfection is off the table. Aim for 'good enough' and celebrate small victories.

6. Prioritize sleep: It might be tempting to use late nights to catch up on chores, but adequate rest will make you more productive overall.

7. Create routines: Establish morning and bedtime routines. They provide structure and can make transitions smoother.

Remember, flexibility is key. Some days, you'll nail it. Other days, it'll feel like you're herding cats. Both are okay. The goal isn't perfection – it's progress.

Here's a little mantra for when things get overwhelming: "I'm doing my best, and my best is enough."

In our next sections, we'll dive deeper into self-care strategies and how to manage the emotional aspects of single parenthood after narcissistic abuse. Remember, you're doing an incredible job juggling it all. Take a moment to appreciate your amazing balancing act!

SELF-CARE ISN'T SELFISH: NURTURING YOUR WELL-BEING

Alright, fantastic parent, let's talk about something super important: YOU. I know, I know - you're probably thinking, "Self-care? I barely have time to shower!" But hear me out. Prioritizing yourself is crucial, especially when you're recovering from narcissistic abuse and single-handedly raising tiny humans.

Self-care doesn't have to mean spa days and yoga retreats (though if you can swing it, go for it!). It's about finding small moments throughout your day to nourish your mind, body, and soul. Here are some ideas:

1. Micro-moments of mindfulness: Take three deep breaths while waiting for your coffee to brew, or do a quick body scan while tucking your kids in.

2. Move your body: Dance in the kitchen while cooking, do some stretches during TV commercials, or have a living room dance party with the kids.

3. Nourish yourself: Prep healthy snacks for yourself when you're making your kids' lunches. Your body deserves fuel too!

4. Connect with others: Schedule a weekly phone date with a friend, join an online support group for single parents, or find a local meetup group.

5. Pursue a passion: Set aside 15 minutes a day for something you love - reading, drawing, knitting, whatever lights you up.

6. Sleep hygiene: Create a relaxing bedtime routine for yourself, just like you do for your kids.

7. Say no: Remember, "No" is a complete sentence. It's okay to set boundaries.

8. Positive self-talk: Challenge negative thoughts. Would you talk to your best friend the way you talk to yourself?

Self-care isn't selfish. By taking care of yourself, you're modeling healthy behavior for your kids and ensuring you have the energy to be the amazing parent you are.

Try this: Create a "Self-Care Emergency Kit." Fill a box with items that soothe or energize you - a favorite tea, a scented candle, a playlist of your favorite songs, a cozy blanket. When you're feeling overwhelmed, take a few minutes to dip into your kit.

EMOTIONAL BALANCING ACT: STAYING STRONG WHILE BEING HUMAN

Let's get real for a moment. Being a single parent after leaving a narcissistic relationship is an emotional rollercoaster. One minute you're feeling strong and empowered, the next you're a puddle of tears over a load of unfolded laundry. Guess what? That's completely normal and absolutely okay.

Your kids don't need you to be perfect. They need you to be present, loving, and real. It's okay to let them see that you're human, that you have emotions, and that you're working through challenges. In fact, by doing so, you're teaching them invaluable lessons about resilience, emotional intelligence, and healthy coping mechanisms.

Here are some strategies for maintaining emotional balance:

1. Acknowledge your feelings: Name your emotions without judgment. "I'm feeling overwhelmed right now, and that's okay."

2. Model healthy expression: Show your kids appropriate ways to

express and manage emotions. "I'm feeling frustrated, so I'm going to take a few deep breaths to calm down."

3. Create a 'feelings check-in' routine: Have regular chats with your kids about emotions. This helps them process their feelings about the family changes and gives you insight into their emotional world.

4. Develop a support network: Have a few trusted friends or family members you can turn to when you need to vent or cry.

5. Seek professional help: There's no shame in talking to a therapist. They can provide tools to manage stress and heal from your past relationship.

6. Practice self-compassion: Treat yourself with the same kindness you'd show a good friend. You're doing the best you can in a challenging situation.

7. Celebrate small victories: Did you get everyone to school on time? Win! Did you manage to eat a vegetable today? Celebration time!

8. Create new family traditions: This helps build a sense of stability and joy in your new family dynamic.

It's okay to have good days and bad days. Your journey of healing isn't smooth and predictable, and that's perfectly normal. What matters is that you're moving forward, one step at a time.

Try this exercise: Start a "Proud Parent Moments" journal. Each day, write down one thing you're proud of as a parent. On tough days, read through your entries. You'll be amazed at how much you're accomplishing.

In our next sections, we'll talk about building your support network and managing finances as a single parent. Remember, you're doing an incredible job navigating this emotional terrain. Your strength and resilience are shaping a beautiful future for you and your children.

Don't be afraid to ask for help. Your village wants to support you - let them!

BUILDING YOUR PARENTING VILLAGE

You've probably heard the saying, "It takes a village to raise a child." As a single parent, it's time to embrace this wisdom and build your own support network. This isn't about admitting defeat; it's about recognizing that humans are social creatures, and we thrive with community support.

Here are some unique ways to build your village:

1. Single Parent Support Groups: Look for local or online groups specifically for single parents. These can be goldmines of emotional support and practical advice from people who truly understand your situation.

2. Skill Swaps: Connect with other parents to trade skills. Maybe you're great at math tutoring but struggle with home repairs. Find a handy parent who needs help with their kid's homework and arrange a skill swap.

3. Childcare Co-ops: Team up with other trusted parents to create a rotating childcare schedule. This can give you much-needed breaks without the financial strain of paid childcare.

4. Virtual Village: In this digital age, don't underestimate the power of online communities. Join forums or social media groups for single parents in your area.

5. Intergenerational Connections: Consider reaching out to older adults in your community, perhaps through a local community center. Many would love to be 'adopted' grandparents and can offer both practical help and wisdom.

Asking for help is a sign of wisdom and strength. You're modeling for your children how to build and maintain supportive relationships.

FINANCIAL FINESSE FOR ONE-INCOME FAMILIES

Navigating finances on a single income can feel like trying to stretch a rubber band across the Grand Canyon. But with some creative strategies, you can create financial stability and even growth.

1. Reassess Your Career: Could you transition to a higher-paying field or negotiate a raise? Many companies are now offering remote work options, which could reduce childcare costs.

2. Explore Passive Income: Consider ways to make money while you sleep. Could you rent out a room on Airbnb? Sell digital products online? Every little bit helps.

3. Teach Financial Literacy: Involve your kids in age-appropriate financial discussions. This not only helps them understand the family's situation but also teaches them valuable life skills.

4. Barter Economy: Get creative with bartering services in your community. From babysitting exchanges to trading professional skills, you'd be surprised what you can accomplish without money changing hands.

5. Minimalism with a Purpose: Embrace minimalism not just as a way to save money, but as a life philosophy. Teach your kids that experiences and relationships are more valuable than things.

6. Government Assistance: Don't shy away from legitimate government assistance programs. These can be a crucial stepping stone as you build financial independence.

CO-PARENTING CHALLENGES: DEALING WITH A NARCISSISTIC EX

Co-parenting with a narcissist brings unique challenges. While we've discussed general co-parenting strategies earlier, here are some specific tips for this situation:

1. Parallel Parenting: When co-parenting proves too difficult, consider parallel parenting. This involves disengaging from your ex and focusing solely on your time with the children.

2. Documentation is Key: Keep meticulous records of all

interactions, agreements, and your ex's behavior. This can be crucial if legal issues arise.

3. Use Technology Wisely: Utilize co-parenting apps for all communication. These provide a recorded, neutral platform for interactions.

4. Emotional Firewall: Create an emotional barrier between you and your ex's behavior. Their actions are a reflection of them, not you.

5. Focus on Your Children: When interactions get tough, remind yourself that it's about your kids, not about winning against your ex.

6. Self-Care After Interactions: Have a self-care routine in place for after you've had to interact with your ex. This helps you decompress and avoid transferring stress to your children. This may include relaxation techniques or journaling.

Your primary goal is to provide a stable, loving environment for your children. You're breaking the cycle of narcissistic abuse, and that's an incredible gift to your kids.

In our final sections, we'll explore how to help your children thrive in this new family dynamic and celebrate your growth as a single parent.

HELPING YOUR CHILDREN THRIVE IN A NEW FAMILY DYNAMIC

Transitioning to a single-parent household after leaving a narcissistic relationship presents unique challenges for children. Here are some strategies to help your kids not just adapt, but flourish:

1. Age-Appropriate Honesty: While we've discussed the importance of open communication, with children of narcissists, it's crucial to help them understand that the family changes aren't their fault. Use age-appropriate language to explain the situation without vilifying their other parent.

2. Emotional Vocabulary Building: Children from narcissistic households often struggle to identify and express emotions. Create an "emotion word of the day" game to expand their emotional vocabulary and awareness.

3. Consistency Amidst Change: Establish new family rituals that are uniquely yours. This could be a special handshake, a weekly game night, or a monthly "adventure day" where you explore new places together.

4. Empowerment Through Choices: Narcissistic households often rob children of agency. Offer age-appropriate choices in daily life to help them regain a sense of control. "Would you like to wear the red shirt or the blue one today?"

5. Praise Effort, Not Just Results: Children of narcissists often feel

they're never good enough. Focus on praising their efforts and progress, not just achievements.

6. Encourage Healthy Relationships: Help your children identify and cultivate healthy friendships. This can serve as a counterbalance to the unhealthy relationship modeled by the narcissistic parent.

7. Mindfulness for Kids: Introduce child-friendly mindfulness exercises. These can help children stay grounded when dealing with a narcissistic parent or processing complex emotions.

8. Create a "Safe Space": Designate a physical space in your home where your child can go when feeling overwhelmed. Stock it with comforting items and calming activities.

Your home is now a safe haven of unconditional love and support. By consistently modeling healthy behaviors and emotions, you're reprogramming your children's understanding of what relationships should look like.

REDISCOVERING YOU: PERSONAL GROWTH AS A SINGLE PARENT

Leaving a narcissistic relationship and embracing single parenthood is not just about survival—it's an opportunity for profound personal growth. Let's explore some unique ways to rediscover and reinvent yourself:

1. Identify and Reclaim Lost Passions: Narcissistic relationships often require you to sideline your own interests. Make a list of

hobbies or passions you gave up and choose one to reintegrate into your life.

2. Challenge Limiting Beliefs: Narcissistic abuse can instill deep-seated limiting beliefs. Identify one belief that's holding you back and actively challenge it this month.

3. Expand Your World: Commit to learning something new that has nothing to do with parenting or your ex. Whether it's a language, a craft, or a scientific topic, expanding your knowledge can be incredibly empowering.

4. Redefine Success: Your definition of success may have been warped by your past relationship. Take time to consciously redefine what success means to you now, as a single parent and individual.

5. Future Self Journaling: Spend 10 minutes each day writing as if you're your ideal future self. What does your life look like? How do you feel? This exercise can help clarify your goals and boost motivation.

6. Personal Board of Directors: Assemble a metaphorical "board of directors" for your life. Choose people (real or historical figures) whose values and achievements you admire. When facing decisions, ask yourself what advice they might offer.

7. Celebrate Autonomy: Recognize the freedom in making decisions without needing to consult or appease a narcissistic

partner. Celebrate this autonomy, even in small choices.

8. Self-Compassion Challenge: For one week, speak to yourself as you would to a dear friend navigating single parenthood after narcissistic abuse. Notice how this shift in self-talk affects your mood and confidence.

CELEBRATING YOUR SINGLE PARENT SUPERPOWERS

As we wrap up this chapter, it's time to acknowledge and celebrate the incredible superpowers you've developed as a single parent recovering from narcissistic abuse:

1. Resilience: You've weathered storms that would have capsized many others. Your ability to bounce back is nothing short of superhuman.

2. Emotional Intelligence: Navigating the complex emotions of both yourself and your children has honed your EQ to expert levels.

3. Efficiency: You've mastered the art of getting things done with limited time and resources. You're the MacGyver of parenting!

4. Boundary-Setting: You've learned to set and maintain healthy boundaries, a crucial skill that many people never master.

5. Adaptability: Life keeps throwing curveballs, and you keep knocking them out of the park. Your adaptability is off the charts.

6. Love Amplification: Despite past hurts, you've expanded your capacity for love, showering your children with the affection and support they need.

7. Intuition: You've learned to trust your gut, especially when it comes to protecting yourself and your children.

8. Personal Growth: You're committed to continual self-improvement, breaking negative cycles and creating a healthier future for your family.

Here's a final exercise to cement your superpowers:

Write a letter to yourself from your children's future adult perspective. Imagine them reflecting on your strength, love, and dedication during these challenging years. What would they say about your superpowers and the impact you've had on their lives?

Remember, incredible parent, you're not just surviving. You're thriving and setting a powerful example for your children. Your journey as a single parent rising from narcissistic abuse is a testament to the strength of the human spirit. Keep nurturing your superpowers, keep growing, and keep celebrating your victories, both big and small. You're not just reclaiming your life; you're creating a beautiful new one. And that, dear reader, is truly super.

CONCLUSION

My dear friend, warrior, survivor - take a deep breath. Feel the strength in your lungs, the power in your heart. You've made it. Not just through this book, but through one of life's most challenging storms. And here you are, still standing, still breathing, still fighting. I am in awe of you.

As we close this chapter of our journey together, know that this book may be ending, but your story - your beautiful, powerful, resilient story - is just beginning its most exciting chapter.

RECAP OF KEY POINTS

Let's take a moment to reflect on how far you've come:

In Chapter 1, we pulled back the curtain on narcissistic abuse, shining a light on the shadows that once left you feeling confused and alone. You now understand that the problem was never you - it was the toxic dynamic you were trapped in.

Chapter 2 validated the hurricane of emotions you've been navigating. Your feelings aren't just valid; they're a testament to your capacity to love, to hope, and yes, to heal.

In Chapter 3, you are armed with tools to protect your mental health. Like a warrior donning armor, you've learned to shield your mind from gaslighting and manipulation.

Chapter 4 guided you through the legal labyrinth of divorce. You're no longer lost in a maze of legal jargon - you're striding forward, informed and empowered.

With Chapter 5, you've reclaimed your financial future. Every budget you make, every financial decision you take, is an act of reclaiming your independence.

Chapter 6 equipped you with strategies for co-parenting with a narcissist. You're breaking cycles and creating a safe, loving environment for your children. Your strength is their strength.

In Chapter 7, your self-esteem is rebuilt brick by brick. Every affirmation, every boundary you set, is a foundation stone in the masterpiece that is you.

Chapter 8 was all about rediscovery. Like an explorer charting new territories, you've begun mapping the landscape of your authentic self.

And in Chapter 9, we looked to the future, turning pain into growth and seeing how others have not just survived, but thrived.

Chapter 10 charts the uncharted waters of single parenthood after narcissistic abuse. Like a skilled captain navigating stormy seas, you've learned to steer your family ship with steady hands and a brave heart. We've explored the unique challenges you face, from juggling multiple roles to creating a safe harbor for your children amidst the turbulence. But more than that, we've discovered the hidden treasures in this journey - the profound personal growth, the strengthening of your parent-child bond, and the creation of a healthier family dynamic. You've not just weathered the storm; you've learned to dance in the rain, turning challenges into opportunities for resilience and love. This chapter celebrates your transformation from a survivor to a thriver, crafting a beautiful new normal for you and your children.

This book isn't the hero of your story. You are.

This book has been your companion, your confidant, your midnight friend when the world felt too dark. But the raw courage it took to reach out and grab this lifeline? The unwavering strength that's kept you turning pages even when your heart felt too heavy to beat? The incredible resilience that's pushed you forward, one word at a time, even on days when breathing felt like a marathon?

That's all you.

Every tear you've shed, every fear you've faced, every small victory you've celebrated – that's the stuff of true heroism. You've walked through fire and come out not just surviving, but ready to thrive. You are the author of your own redemption story, the architect of your new beginning, the painter of your brighter tomorrow.

When you close this book and catch your reflection, see this: a person of immense courage, boundless strength, and awe-inspiring resilience. A true hero.

Your journey isn't over. There will still be tough days, moments of doubt, times when the past feels too heavy. But now you have the tools, the knowledge, and most importantly, the self-awareness to navigate whatever comes your way. Remember, you're more than capable of handling this journey. And on the days when doubt creeps in and you feel overwhelmed, take heart in knowing a whole community of survivors is rallying behind you, cheering you on every step of the way. You're never flying solo on this path to healing and empowerment.

You picked up this book because some part of you, no matter how small, believed in the possibility of a better future. Hold onto that belief. Nurture it. Watch it grow. Your ex-partner tried to write your story for you, but this is your pen now. You get to write the next chapters, and they're going to be a masterpiece.

If this book has helped you rediscover your strength, rekindled your hope, or simply made you feel less isolated in your journey, then pay it forward. Share your story. Be the guiding light that helps another survivor find their path out of the darkness.

WORDS OF ENCOURAGEMENT

Before we part ways, here are some words of encouragement. Think of these as your north star - guiding lights to turn to when the path seems dark or uncertain.

1. You are stronger than you know. The very fact that you're here, reading these words, is proof of your incredible strength. You've survived the unimaginable, and that resilience will carry you forward.

2. Your worth is not determined by others. No matter what your narcissistic ex may have told you, your value is intrinsic. It doesn't depend on anyone's approval or validation. You are worthy of love, respect, and happiness, simply because you exist.

3. You deserve peace and joy. After the storm you've weathered, you might feel guilty for wanting happiness. Don't. You've earned every moment of peace and every burst of joy that comes your way. Embrace them fully.

4. Your past does not define your future. What happened to you is part of your story, but it's not the whole story. Your future is unwritten, full of possibilities. You have the power to shape it.

5. Healing is not linear. Some days will feel like two steps forward, others like one step back. That's okay. Healing is a journey, not a destination. Every step, no matter the direction, is progress.

6. You are not alone. Even in your darkest moments, remember that there's a whole community of survivors out there who understand. Reach out. Connect. Let their strength bolster yours.

7. Your voice matters. You might have been silenced in the past, but your voice is powerful. Use it. Share your story. Your words could

be the lifeline another survivor needs.

8. It's okay to put yourself first. Self-care isn't selfish. It's necessary. Prioritizing your well-being isn't just okay - it's essential for your healing journey.

9. Small steps lead to big changes. Don't underestimate the power of small actions. Each boundary you set, each self-affirming thought, each moment of self-care is a victory. Celebrate these wins.

10. You have everything you need within you. The strength, the wisdom, the resilience to heal and thrive - it's all already within you. This book may have helped you access it, but it was always there.

11. Your vulnerability is your strength. Opening up about your experiences, allowing yourself to feel, to heal - that takes immense courage. Your vulnerability is not weakness; it's your greatest strength.

12. The best is yet to come. I know it might be hard to believe right now, but your best days are ahead of you. You're not just surviving anymore; you're preparing to thrive.

Healing is not about becoming a new person. It's about unveiling the strong, beautiful soul that was always there, beneath the layers of abuse and self-doubt. It's about reclaiming your life, your joy, your power.

As you close this book and step forward into your new chapter, carry these words with you. Let them be your mantra, your battle cry, your lullaby - whatever you need them to be in the moment.

RESOURCES FOR ONGOING SUPPORT: YOUR HEALING TOOLKIT

As you continue on your journey of healing and self-discovery, know that support is always available. Here's a curated list of resources to help you along the way:

Hotlines and Crisis Support

1. **National Domestic Violence Hotline**

   - Phone: 1-800-799-SAFE (7233)
   - Website: www.thehotline.org
   - 24/7 support for crisis intervention, safety planning, and referrals

2. **Crisis Text Line**

   - Text HOME to 741741
   - 24/7 support via text for any type of crisis

Therapy and Counseling

1. **Psychology Today Therapist Finder**

   - Website: www.psychologytoday.com/us/therapists
   - Search for therapists specializing in narcissistic abuse recovery in your area

2. **BetterHelp**

    - Website: www.betterhelp.com

    - Online counseling platform with licensed therapists

Support Groups

1. **Narcissistic Abuse Support**

    - Website: www.narcissisticabusesupport.com

    - Online support groups and resources

2. **CODA (Co-Dependents Anonymous)**

    - Website: www.coda.org

    - 12-step program for recovery from codependency

Legal Resources

1. **WomensLaw.org**

    - Website: www.womenslaw.org

    - Legal information and resources for women facing abuse

2. **American Bar Association - Commission on Domestic & Sexual Violence**

    - Website: www.americanbar.org/groups/domestic_violence

- Resources and referrals for legal assistance

Financial Advice

1. **National Foundation for Credit Counseling**

    - Website: www.nfcc.org
    - Financial education and counseling services

2. **Women's Institute for Financial Education (WIFE)**

    - Website: www.wife.org
    - Financial education specifically for women

Books and Podcasts

1. **"Psychopath Free" by Jackson MacKenzie**

    - A healing guide for survivors of toxic relationships

2. **"The Narcissist in Your Life" podcast by Linda Martinez-Lewi**

    - Insights and strategies for dealing with narcissistic relationships

Self-Care and Healing Apps

1. **Calm**

    - Meditation and mindfulness app to help manage stress and

anxiety

2. **Moodfit**

- Tools for tracking mood and developing coping strategies

Online Communities

1. **Reddit r/NarcissisticAbuse**

- Subreddit: www.reddit.com/r/NarcissisticAbuse

- Supportive online community for survivors of narcissistic abuse

2. **Out of the FOG Forum**

- Website: outofthefog.website/forum

- Online forum for those dealing with personality-disordered individuals

These resources are here to support, guide, and remind you that you're part of a community of survivors and thrivers.

As you explore these resources, be patient with yourself. Healing is a personal journey, and what works for one person may not work for another. Feel free to try different options until you find the support that resonates with you.

Know you are worthy of support. You are deserving of healing. Your journey to reclaiming your life is important, and there are countless people and resources ready to support you along the way.

Keep this list handy, and don't hesitate to reach out when you need support. Your healing journey continues, and with these resources, you're well-equipped for the path ahead.

ADDITIONAL TOOLS

A COMPREHENSIVE JOURNAL

This journal is your trusted companion on this incredible journey you're embarking on. Think of it as a dear friend who's always ready to listen, a cheerleader to celebrate your victories (big and small!), and a gentle guide to help you navigate the tougher days.

In these pages, you have the freedom to be entirely, unabashedly you. Whether you prefer writing long, heartfelt entries, jotting down quick thoughts, doodling your feelings, or making lists – this space is yours to use in whatever way serves you best.

Each section of this journal aligns with a chapter. You'll find a variety of prompts, exercises, and reflection points for each chapter. Feel free to pick and choose what resonates with you on any given day – there's no "right" way to use this journal.

JOURNAL

Daily Check-In Page

Quick Daily Check-In

Date: _____

Today I feel: (Circle all that apply or add your own)

_____

One word to describe my day: _____

Something I'm grateful for: _____

One kind thing I did for myself: _____

Daily Reflection

Date: _____

My energy level today (1-10): ___

Three emotions I experienced today:

    1. _____

    2. _____

    3. _____

Three things I'm grateful for:

1. _____

2. _____

3. _____

A challenge I faced today:

_____

How I handled it:

_____

Something I'm proud of:

_____

A positive affirmation for tomorrow:

_____

Additional thoughts or reflections:

_____

_____

_____

Healing Milestones

Use these pages to record moments of breakthrough, realizations, or achievements. Remember, every step forward is a victory, no matter how small it might seem!

Date: _____

Milestone: _____

Reflection: _____

Date: _____

Milestone: _____

Reflection: _____

Date: _____

Milestone: _____

Reflection: _____

PROGRESS TRACKER

Healing is a process, and it's important to acknowledge how far you've come. Use this tracker to celebrate your progress:

Monthly Check-In:

Date: _____

On a scale of 1-10:

- My overall well-being: ____

- My sense of self-worth: ____

- My ability to set boundaries: ____

- My hope for the future: ____

Three ways I've grown this month:

1. _____
2. _____
3. _____

One challenge I've overcome:

_____

Something I'm proud of:

_____

My goal for next month:

_____

Be patient with yourself and celebrate every step forward, no matter how small!

REFLECTION POINTS

Chapter 1: Understanding Narcissistic Abuse

- Abuse Recognition:
  - What behaviors am I now recognizing as abusive that I might have overlooked before?
  - How did these behaviors impact me emotionally, mentally, and physically?
  - What patterns do I see in these behaviors?

- Emotional Exploration:
  - How do I feel as I gain this new understanding about narcissistic abuse?
  - If these feelings were colors, what would they be and why?
  - Write a letter to your past self, sharing what you've learned about narcissistic abuse.

- Personal Strength Inventory:
  - What strengths have I discovered in myself through this experience?
  - How have these strengths helped me survive and cope?
  - In what ways can I continue to nurture these strengths?

- Moving Forward:
  - What boundaries do I need to set now that I understand narcissistic abuse better?
  - How can I use this knowledge to protect myself in future relationships?
  - What support do I need as I process this new understanding?

Chapter 2: The Emotional Toll of Divorce from a Narcissist

- Emotion Mapping:
  - How am I really feeling today about my divorce?
  - Create a 'map' of your emotional journey so far. What have been the major landmarks?
  - If your emotions were weather patterns, what would today's forecast be?

- Challenging Emotions:
  - What's the hardest emotion I'm dealing with right now?
  - Where do I feel this emotion in my body?
  - If this emotion could speak, what would it say?

- Self-Compassion Practice:
  - What's one small way I can show myself compassion today?

- Write a loving message to yourself as if you were your own best friend.
- How can I honor my feelings without being overwhelmed by them?

- Grief and Growth:
  - What losses am I grieving in this divorce process?
  - What unexpected positive changes have occurred since my divorce?
  - How has this experience changed my view of myself and relationships?

Chapter 3: Protecting Your Mental Health

- Self-Care Exploration:
  - What self-care activities make me feel most at peace?
  - How can I incorporate more of these activities into my daily routine?
  - Create a 'menu' of self-care options for different moods or situations.

- Boundary Setting:
  - What boundaries do I need to set or reinforce?

- How will I communicate these boundaries to others?

- What might make it challenging to maintain these boundaries, and how can I prepare for that?

- Mindfulness and Grounding:

  - Describe a place where you feel safe and peaceful. Use all your senses.

  - Try a 5-minute mindfulness exercise. How do you feel before and after?

  - List 5 grounding techniques that work for you in moments of stress or anxiety.

- Negative Thought Patterns:

  - What negative thoughts do I often have about myself?

  - How can I challenge and reframe these thoughts?

  - Write a compassionate response to your most common negative thought.

Chapter 4: Navigating the Legal Process

- Legal Journey Mapping:

  - What aspects of the legal process are most confusing or stressful for me?

- Create a timeline of the legal process ahead. What are the key milestones?

- How can I break down this process into more manageable steps?

- Preparation and Empowerment:

  - How can I better prepare myself for upcoming legal proceedings?

  - What questions do I need to ask my lawyer?

  - Write a personal mantra or affirmation for strength during legal meetings.

- Support System:

  - What support do I need during this process, and who can I ask for help?

  - How can I create a self-care routine specifically for legal stress?

  - Write a letter to your support system, expressing your needs and gratitude.

- Emotional Processing:

  - How do I feel before, during, and after interactions with the legal system?

  - What coping strategies can I use to manage stress during this process?

- Reflect on a recent legal hurdle you overcame. How did you manage it?

Chapter 5: Financial Survival and Recovery

- Financial Reality Check:
    - What are my biggest financial concerns right now?
    - Create a list of all your current financial resources and liabilities.
    - How has my financial situation changed, and how do I feel about these changes?

- Steps to Stability:
    - What's one step I can take today towards financial stability?
    - Break down your financial goals into small, achievable actions.
    - What skills or resources do I need to develop for better financial management?

- Money Mindset:
    - How has my relationship with money changed, and how do I want it to be?
    - What financial beliefs or habits do I need to change?

- Write a positive affirmation about your financial future.

- Financial Self-Care:

  - How can I balance frugality with self-care?

  - List 5 free or low-cost activities that bring you joy.

  - How can I celebrate financial wins, no matter how small?

Chapter 6: Co-Parenting with a Narcissist

- Co-Parenting Challenges:

  - What challenges am I facing in co-parenting today?

  - How do these challenges affect me emotionally?

  - What strategies have worked well in dealing with my co-parent?

- Child-Centric Focus:

  - How am I putting my children's needs first, even when it's difficult?

  - Write a letter to your children about your commitment to them (you don't have to send it).

  - How can I create a peaceful environment for my children amidst the co-parenting conflict?

- Communication Strategies:

- What techniques help me communicate effectively with my co-parent?

- Draft a template for business-like communication with your co-parent.

- How can I set and maintain clear boundaries in co-parenting interactions?

- Self-Care in Co-Parenting:

  - What strategies help me stay calm during interactions with my ex?

  - How can I decompress after difficult co-parenting situations?

  - List 5 self-care activities specifically for co-parenting stress relief.

Chapter 7: Rebuilding Your Self-Esteem

- Self-Appreciation:

  - What's one thing I like about myself today?

  - List 10 of your positive qualities. How have these helped you in your journey?

  - Write about a time when you felt truly proud of yourself.

- Growth and Strength:

- How have I grown stronger through this experience?
- What challenges have I overcome that I never thought I could?
- How can I celebrate my resilience and courage?

- Challenging Negative Self-Talk:
  - What negative self-talk do I need to challenge and change?
  - For each negative thought, write a compassionate, realistic counter-thought.
  - Create a list of personal affirmations that resonate with you.

- Future Self:
  - Write a letter from your future self, describing how far you've come.
  - What new beliefs about yourself do you want to cultivate?
  - How can you start treating yourself with the respect and love you deserve?

Chapter 8: Rediscovering Yourself

- Authentic Self-Exploration:
  - What activities or interests make me feel most like "me"?
  - How have my passions or interests changed since my relationship ended?

- If I could do anything without fear of judgment, what would it be?

- New Experiences:
  - What's one new thing I'd like to try this week?
  - List 5 activities or skills you've always wanted to explore.
  - How can I step out of my comfort zone in a small way today?

- Identity Reflection:
  - How has my idea of who I am changed since my divorce?
  - What parts of myself did I lose in my relationship that I want to reclaim?
  - Create a vision board (in words or images) of the life you want to create.

- Values and Priorities:
  - What are my top 5 personal values?
  - How can I align my daily life more closely with these values?
  - What new traditions or rituals would I like to create for myself?

Chapter 9: Healing and Moving Forward

- Defining Healing:

- What does "healing" mean to me today?
- How will I know when I've made progress in my healing journey?
- Write a letter to your pain, acknowledging its purpose and releasing it.

- Future Focus:
  - What's one thing I'm looking forward to in my future?
  - Describe your ideal life 5 years from now. What steps can you take towards it?
  - What new opportunities have opened up for me post-divorce?

- Celebrating Progress:
  - How can I celebrate the progress I've made, no matter how small?
  - List 10 ways you've grown or changed positively through this experience.
  - Write a thank-you note to yourself for all you've overcome.

- Lessons and Growth:
  - What are the most important lessons I've learned from this experience?

- How have these lessons changed my perspective on life and relationships?

- In what ways do I want to use my experience to help others?

GLOSSARY OF TERMS

1. Alimony: Financial support paid by one spouse to another after divorce, typically when there's a significant difference in incomes.

2. Asset Division: The process of dividing marital property and debts during a divorce.

3. Child Support: Regular payments made by a non-custodial parent to support their child's living expenses.

4. Cognitive Dissonance: The mental discomfort experienced when a person holds two or more contradictory beliefs, ideas, or values.

5. Custody (Legal and Physical): Legal custody refers to the right to make important decisions about a child's upbringing. Physical custody refers to where the child primarily resides.

6. Deposition: A sworn out-of-court testimony used to gather information as part of the discovery process.

7. Devaluation: The phase in a narcissistic relationship where the narcissist begins to belittle and criticize their partner.

8. Discovery: The formal process of exchanging information between parties about the witnesses and evidence they'll present at trial.

9. Emotional Dysregulation: Difficulty in controlling or regulating emotional responses.

10. Equitable Distribution: A method of dividing marital property that aims for fairness but not necessarily equality.

11. Flying Monkeys: People who act on behalf of a narcissist, often to gather information or to manipulate others.

12. Gaslighting: A form of psychological manipulation where a person makes someone question their own sanity, perception, memories, or judgment.

13. Gray Rock Method: A technique for dealing with narcissists by becoming as reactive and uninteresting as a "gray rock."

14. Hoovering: Attempts by a narcissist to draw a former partner back into a relationship after a period of separation.

15. Love Bombing: An attempt to influence a person by demonstrations of attention and affection. It's often used by narcissists to manipulate their targets.

16. Mediation: A process where a neutral third party helps divorcing

couples negotiate their differences and reach a settlement.

17. Narcissistic Personality Disorder (NPD): A mental condition characterized by an inflated sense of self-importance, a deep need for excessive attention and admiration, and a lack of empathy for others.

18. Narcissistic Supply: The attention, admiration, or emotional energy that narcissists need to fuel their ego and sense of self-importance.

19. No Contact: A strategy of completely ending communication with a narcissistic ex-partner to aid in healing and recovery.

20. No-Fault Divorce: A divorce in which neither party is required to prove wrongdoing by the other.

21. Parentification: A form of role reversal where a child is obliged to act as parent to their own parent or sibling.

22. Parenting Plan: A detailed, written agreement that outlines how parents will raise their children after divorce.

23. Post-Traumatic Growth: Positive psychological change experienced as a result of adversity and other challenges. It often involves a greater appreciation for life, more meaningful relationships, increased personal strength, recognition of new possibilities, and spiritual development.

24. Post-Traumatic Stress Disorder (PTSD): A mental health

condition triggered by experiencing or witnessing a terrifying event. Symptoms may include flashbacks, nightmares, severe anxiety, and uncontrollable thoughts about the event.

25. Postnuptial Agreement: A contract created after marriage that outlines how assets would be divided in case of divorce.

26. Prenuptial Agreement: A contract created before marriage that outlines how assets would be divided in case of divorce.

27. Projection: A defense mechanism where a person attributes their own unacceptable thoughts or behaviors to someone else.

28. Qualified Domestic Relations Order (QDRO): A special court order that allows the division of certain types of retirement plans in a divorce.

29. Restraining Order: A court order that requires a party to do, or refrain from doing, certain acts. In divorce cases, it's often used to prevent harassment or asset dissipation.

30. Scapegoat: A person who is blamed for the wrongdoings, mistakes, or faults of others, especially within a family dynamic.

31. Spousal Support: Another term for alimony.

32. Trauma Bond: A psychological response to abuse where the victim develops an unhealthy attachment to their abuser.

REFERENCES

Arabi, S. (2016). *Becoming the Narcissist's Nightmare: How to Devalue and Discard the Narcissist While Supplying Yourself.* CreateSpace Independent Publishing Platform.

American Bar Association. (2022). *The Divorce Trial Manual: From Initial Interview to Closing Argument.* ABA Book Publishing.

Banschick, M. (2022). *The Intelligent Divorce: Taking Care of Your Children.* Intelligent Book Press.

Behrens, M. W. (2021). *Divorce and Money: How to Make the Best Financial Decisions During Divorce.* Nolo.

Brown, B. (2018). *Dare to Lead: Brave Work. Tough Conversations. Whole Hearts.* Random House.

Cheong, C. Y., & Slotter, E. B. (2021). "Financial Toxicity of Divorce: A Scoping Review." *Journal of Financial Therapy,* 12(1), 4.

Dateline, S. (2020). The High-Conflict Custody Battle: Protect Yourself and Your Kids from a Toxic Divorce, False Accusations, and Parental Alienation. New Harbinger Publications.

Durvasula, R. S. (2019). "Don't You Know Who I Am?": How to Stay Sane in an Era of Narcissism, Entitlement, and Incivility. Post Hill Press.

Eddy, B. (2020). High Conflict People in Legal Disputes. Unhooked Books.

Eddy, B. (2021). Why Does He Do That?: Inside the Minds of Angry and Controlling Men. Berkley.

Evans, P. (2022). The Verbally Abusive Relationship, Expanded Third Edition: How to Recognize It and How to Respond. Adams Media.

Felder, R. & Victor, B. (2021). The Good Divorce: How to Walk Away Financially Sound and Emotionally Happy. St. Martin's Griffin.

Fisher, H. E., & Alberti, R. (2016). Rebuilding: When Your Relationship Ends. Impact Publishers.

Forward, S., & Frazier, D. (2019). Emotional Blackmail: When the People in Your Life Use Fear, Obligation, and Guilt to Manipulate You. William Morrow Paperbacks.

Freyd, J. J., & Birrell, P. J. (2013). Blind to Betrayal: Why We Fool Ourselves We Aren't Being Fooled. John Wiley & Sons.

Gordon, B. (2019). Love, Money, and the Law: A Guide to Building a Family and Protecting Your Assets. Advantage Media Group.

Gottman, J., & Silver, N. (2015). The Seven Principles for Making Marriage Work: A Practical Guide from the Country's Foremost Relationship Expert. Harmony.

Herman, J. L. (2015). Trauma and Recovery: The Aftermath of Violence--From Domestic Abuse to Political Terror. Basic Books.

Hoffman, D. A., & Wolman, R. N. (2012). "The Psychology of Mediation." Cardozo Journal of Conflict Resolution, 14, 759.

Jaffe, P. G., Johnston, J. R., Crooks, C. V., & Bala, N. (2008). "Custody Disputes Involving Allegations of Domestic Violence: Toward a Differentiated Approach to Parenting Plans." Family Court Review, 46(3), 500-522.

Levine, A., & Heller, R. (2012). Attached: The New Science of Adult Attachment and How It Can Help You Find - and Keep - Love. Penguin. 22. Linehan, M. M. (2014). DBT Skills Training Manual, Second Edition. The Guilford Press.

Malkin, C. (2015). Rethinking Narcissism: The Bad - and Surprising Good - About Feeling Special. HarperCollins.

McBride, K. (2018). Will I Ever Be Free of You?: How to Navigate a High-Conflict Divorce from a Narcissist and Heal Your Family. Atria Books.

Payson, E. (2019). The Wizard of Oz and Other Narcissists: Coping with the One-Way Relationship in Work, Love, and Family. Julian Day Publications.

Rosenberg, M. B. (2015). Nonviolent Communication: A Language of Life. PuddleDancer Press.

Saeed, K. (2020). 30 Covert Emotional Manipulation Tactics: How Manipulators Take Control in Personal Relationships. Independently published.

Walker, P. (2013). Complex PTSD: From Surviving to Thriving: A Guide and Map for Recovering from Childhood Trauma. Azure Coyote.

Woodhouse, B. B. (2020). The Ecology of Childhood: How Our Changing World Threatens Children's Rights. NYU Press.

www.ingramcontent.com/pod-product-compliance
Lightning Source LLC
Chambersburg PA
CBHW052154220526
45471CB00004B/1667